THE BOOK OF
MERE

THE BOOK OF
MERE

Portrait of a Wiltshire Town

DR DAVID LONGBOURNE

HALSGROVE

First published in Great Britain in 2004

Title page: *The Square, c.1922.*

British Library Cataloguing-in-Publication Data.
A CIP record for this title is available from the British Library.

ISBN 1 84114 346 4

HALSGROVE

Halsgrove House
Lower Moor Way
Tiverton, Devon EX16 6SS
Tel: 01884 243242
Fax: 01884 243325
email: sales@halsgrove.com
website: www.halsgrove.com

Printed and bound in Great Britain by CPI Bath.

Whilst every care has been taken to ensure the accuracy of the information contained in this book, the publisher disclaims responsibility for any mistakes which may have been inadvertently included.

A charabanc party from Mere.

CONTENTS

ACKNOWLEDGEMENTS

I have enjoyed writing this book but it would not have been possible without the researches done by Michael Tighe to whom I am greatly indebted for allowing me to quote from his series of booklets entitled *Mere Papers* and for proofreading my text. I have, with permission, used a great deal of the material from *The Story of Mere* (1958) and *Mere: A Wiltshire Country Town* (1975) and my thanks go to Norah Rutter who was closely involved in both publications.

The following have kindly contributed information about various voluntary organisations in Mere: Miss M. Burden, Mrs J. Coward, Mrs M. Durkee, Mr G. Edwards, Mrs K. Herbert, Mrs A. Howell, Mrs T. Ings, Mr B. James, Mr D. Lawley, Mrs S. Luffman, Miss B. Naylor, Mr G. Pickford, Mrs G. Pope, Mrs T. Read, Mrs W. Richardson, Mr R. Sheppard, Mr A. Taylor, Mrs J. Young.

I am grateful to Revd Ben Elliott for his comments on my description of St Michael's Church, to Roy Canham, County Archaeologist for Wiltshire, for permission to quote from *The Archaeology of Wiltshire's Towns* by P. McMahon, to Jim Allbrook for use of his monograph on *The History of Zeals Airfield and Aircraft Crashes around Mere, 1939–45*, to Gwyn Jackson for allowing me to quote from the book *A Tale of Two Manors; Zeals, a Wiltshire Village* and to Geraldine Marchand and Colin Anderson for their drawings.

The following have contributed their excellent photographs: Dr C. Anderson, Mrs J. Barnard, Mr M. Head, Mr E. Horan, Dr M. Plaxton, Mr G. Swanson, Mr D. Wilson and I have been able to use photographs from the collections of Salisbury Museum, Wiltshire, as well as Gillingham Museum, Dorset, The National Monuments Record, Swindon, and The Friends of St Michael the Archangel, Mere.

I would like to thank Dr Jenny Wilding, Hon. Assistant Museum Curator at Mere for her help and to Mere Museum Committee for permission to dig deeply into the museum's photographic archive for the majority of the pictures in this book.

Finally, I would like to congratulate the publishers for their enterprise in suggesting that this history of Mere should be written and for the expert advice of Naomi Cudmore, Katy Charge and their colleagues at Halsgrove.

David Longbourne
March 2004

Chapter 1

✧

Landscape and Geology

Mere lies in the south-west corner of Wiltshire with the higher land of Salisbury Plain to the north and east, low-lying pasture land of Dorset to the south and the wooded, gently rolling hills of Somerset to the west. Two miles to the north-west of Mere is Stourhead House with its magnificent and famous gardens. Much of the land in and around Mere is owned by the Duchy of Cornwall and this has had a profound effect on the development of this 'town with a village-like atmosphere'.

The geology of the area around Mere is of particular importance; to the north is a layer of chalk, to the west is upper greensand and to the south, Kimmeridge clay. Where the clay meets the chalk and greensand is the east–west Mere Fault, which

follows a line parallel with the main road; the road keeping to the surer foundation of chalk rather than to the softer clay. Along this line numerous springs occur. At Ashfield, at the bottom of Charnage Hill, surface springs can be seen; at Wellhead they are less obvious but streams from both sources join to form the River Shreen which flows on to Gillingham to become the River Stour.

The chalk escarpment to the north of Mere rises to a height of 802ft at Whitesheet Castle. It is indented with several combes or downland valleys, Great Bottom being the largest; indeed this may be the largest in any chalk escarpment in the country. Other combes to the east of it are Chetcombe Bottom, Ancombe Bottom and Ashfield Bottom and the

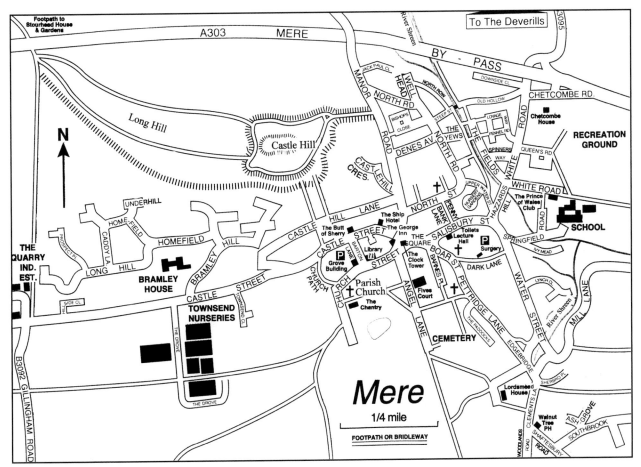

Town map of Mere.

REPRODUCED WITH THE PERMISSION OF MERE INFORMATION CENTRE

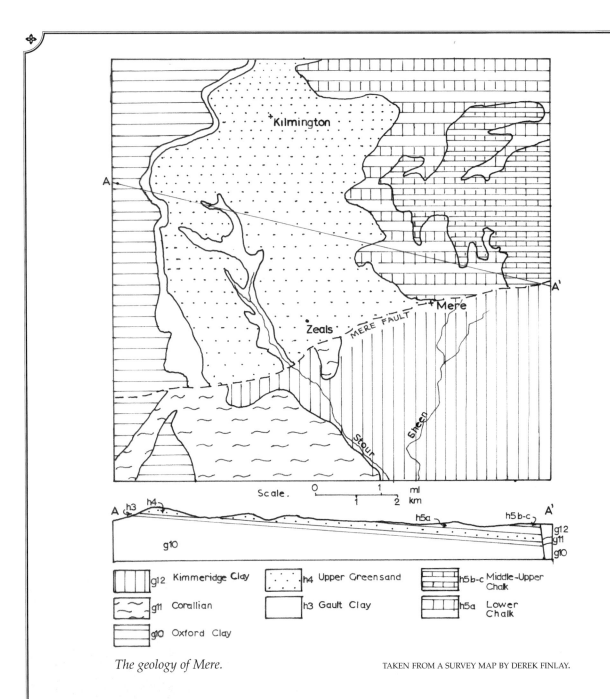

Scale.

| | 0 | | 1 | ml |
| | | 1 | 2 | km |

A h3 h4 h5a h5b-c A'
g12
g11
g10
g10

	g12 Kimmeridge Clay		h4 Upper Greensand		h5b-c Middle-Upper Chalk
	g11 Corallian		h3 Gault Clay		h5a Lower Chalk
	g10 Oxford Clay				

The geology of Mere.

TAKEN FROM A SURVEY MAP BY DEREK FINLAY.

Wolverton Quarry.

Chalkpit at Charnage.

slopes of these valleys are terraced with lynchets (ridges formed through ancient ploughing) of great antiquity.

Many of the houses and walls in Mere were built with the local stone from Dead Maid Quarry at the western edge of the town. Chloritic marl, Warminster greensand and upper greensand provided much of this stone and the greenish sandstone from an underground quarry at Wolverton may have been used in the building of Mere Parish Church. This quarry is thought to have been worked not later than the twelfth or thirteenth century. Some houses in the town contain a few blocks of greenish stone which may well have been robbed from the ruined Mere Castle.

Chalk for agricultural purposes is quarried on the eastern side of Mere at Charnage and flints used to be quarried from the downs for road making.

Whitesheet Hill.

So it is that the geology has influenced the scenery, the architecture, the industry, the agriculture, the trees, birds and varied flora of downland, meadow, wood and river in Mere and its surrounding country.

Aerial view of Mere, 1978.

Chapter 2

Early History

Mere and its neighbouring hamlets are good examples of 'spring line settlements'. We have seen in Chapter 1 that where the Kimmeridge clay to the south of Mere meets the porous chalk of the downs to the north, numerous springs occur. The chalk downs favoured early settlement presumably for reasons of safety but they suffered from an absence of water; so the abundance of water along the Mere Fault must have encouraged further settlement there. In the heavy waterlogged soil to the south of Mere there are two low ridges running southwards: the Causeway heading towards Shaftesbury and the line of the Gillingham Road, both of which would have provided reasonably reliable routes into Dorset.

Settlements would also have been likely on the better drained land on the greensand which runs southwards from Norton Ferris, Kilmington, and Stourton to Zeals. A narrow tongue of this greensand runs right into the town along the line of Castle Street and the soils in the town vary over very short distances between chalk, sand and heavy clay. The clay contains occasional veins of 'white earth', a chalky loam with some flint which is an erosion product from the downs. This was once used for cottage floors and even the church was once floored with it. In 1879 workmen digging a trench at The Lynch struck a vein of mica which caused some excitement for local geologists; it has not been found elsewhere in Mere as far as is known.

There is abundant evidence of settlements dating from all prehistoric periods on the chalk downs to the north of Mere but this does not mean that there were no settlements on the lower land, although evidence

Aerial view of Whitesheet Castle.

for it is scanty. Mesolithic flint cores were found during the construction of Mere bypass in 1975 and Neolithic artefacts have been found in and around Mere. A group of four bowl barrows has been located on Castle Hill; there is another barrow at Burton and one at The Middles, West Knoyle, was used many centuries later as the base for a windmill. Sir Richard Colt Hoare of Stourhead, writing in the early-nineteenth century, recorded the finding of a number of low barrows at Mappledore Hill on the Gillingham Road and in cutting a ditch through one of them some vessels of coarse pottery were found. A chipped flint axe was found in Manor Road and is now in Mere Museum. Bronze palstaves (axes) were discovered at Woodlands Manor and on Long Hill and a socketed axe at Charnage. Also at Charnage, Roman jewellery and coins were found and in 1856 a jar containing a hoard of 270 Roman denarii of varying kinds dating from AD65 to AD166 was unearthed when drainage trenches were being dug out in Mere Cemetery in Angel Lane. With the discovery of Bronze-Age artefacts in various parts of the lowland area we are justified in assuming that there probably was some sort of Bronze-Age settlement in Mere.

On the higher ground to the north of Mere the most spectacular survival of downland settlement is the hill-fort of Whitesheet Castle. Here are the remains of a Neolithic (c.3,000BC) causewayed camp and around it a number of barrows of the Bronze Age (c.2,000BC). The site was further fortified in the Iron Age (c.500BC) and there are now three ditches and ramparts with staggered entrances on the eastern side. During the Iron Age Mere seems to have lain within the territory of the Durotridges, a confederation of people occupying all of Dorset and most of Wiltshire. Of this period, a bronze brooch was found at Charnage Down and an inscribed gold coin of the Durotridges found elsewhere in the parish. Of the finds in excavated barrows, a large urn was in a bowl barrow on Whitesheet Hill, a smaller urn with perforated lugs was in a bowl barrow on Charnage Down and a beaker, a tanged dagger, the slate wrist guard of an archer, a bone implement and two gold discs came from a barrow on Mere Down. There is evidence of ancient field systems west of Mere Down House and at Charnage Down; these arable plots of the Iron Age were likely to have grown wheat, barley, oats and rye. An iron spearhead from Charnage, a bronze bowl, wooden bucket, shield bars, spears, knives, buckles, and a clasp and sword from a barrow on Rodmead Hill to the north-east of Whitesheet all belong to the fifth and sixth centuries AD.

Running across the top of Whitesheet Hill and Mere Down is a prehistoric trackway, a ridgeway, which until the mid-eighteenth century was one of the major roads to the west of England. There are milestones along it dated 1750 but when the Wincanton Turnpike was established in 1758, the road to the west moved down into Mere itself.

The old trackway on Mere Down.

Strip lynchets at Mere.

The Chantry pond, south of the Parish Church, 1987.

The trackway is said to have been used to drive sheep and cattle to the fairs at Wilton and Salisbury and for transporting lead from mines in the Mendips.

This region came under the control of the Romans following the invasion of AD43 when the subjugation of the West was undertaken by Vespasian. It was subsequently garrisoned and service roads were constructed, some of them following existing trackways – indeed, the Mere trackway may have been one of them. However, there is a known Roman road through Kingston Deverill with a minor one running southwards from it through East Knoyle to Poole, so Roman presence in the Mere area is doubtful.

Below the Mere Down trackway and on the eastern side of the town are the three deep combes or valleys in the chalk downs mentioned in Chapter 1 as having on their sides strip lynchets. These lynchets are sometimes thought to be Anglo-Saxon in origin but that steep hillsides covered by only a thin layer of soil should have been used at all is surprising. Perhaps the poorer people were denied the use of the available lower ground and were forced to find an alternative on the hillsides. The strip lynchets are similar to the terraces the Romans used for growing vines but there is nothing to suggest any Roman origin for them.

Anglo-Saxon settlement came to Wiltshire in about AD500 but in Mere, remains of this period are very few indeed. Across the Dorset border at Gillingham there is evidence of Romano-British and Saxon settlement and nearby Shaftesbury was an important Saxon town. However, in 1995, workmen repairing a wall in Barnes Place, Mere, came upon the skeleton of a young woman with three pieces of fine jewellery beside her and this has been identified as a seventh-century Saxon burial. The jewellery is now on display in Salisbury Museum. Another skeleton had been found on the west side of Water Street 12

Saxon jewellery found at Mere in 1995. (PHOTOGRAPH REPRODUCED WITH THE PERMISSION OF SALISBURY MUSEUM)

years earlier and was thought to be a Saxon burial. In Mere Parish Church there is, at the west end of the nave, a wall which the architect C.E. Ponting believed to be part of an original Saxon church. So, although the evidence is slight, a Saxon settlement seems likely.

The town's name is of Saxon origin but two explanations for it have been put forward. The great antiquary Aubrey said that the name derives from *maera* meaning march or boundary and as Mere is situated near the meeting place of three counties and as England was shired in Saxon times, he was probably right. It is known that the pre-Roman tribal borders and later divisions ran along the line of the old Selwood Forest. Nevertheless, the name has a watery connotation and as there is an ancient pond to the south of the Parish Church, it could equally easily refer to this. Whichever derivation is the right one, Mere was most likely to have been a Saxon frontier settlement with a good supply of water.

Castle Hill, St Michael's Church and The Chantry from the south-west.

Chapter 3

Medieval Mere and the Castle

After a meeting of the witan – an assembly of higher churchmen and important laymen who advised the King – during the Christmas season of 1085 it was decided that a description of the kingdom, 'how it was occupied and with what sort of men' should be prepared. Wiltshire and the four south-western shires appear to have been assigned to a single body of commissioners and the survey was begun in 1086. The information gathered by the commissioners was entered into the *Exchequer Domesday, Volume 1*. More detailed information about livestock and other matters regarded of lesser importance is found in the *Exon Domesday* (Exon refers to Exeter where the volume was kept).

In the survey the term 'hide' is used as a measure of area and this was anything from 60 to 100 acres; the variation can be explained by the fact that as this undertaking was mainly for taxation purposes, the hide was a measurement of land value, i.e. the amount of land needed for the support of one family with its dependents or the land that could be tilled by one plough team of eight oxen if the land was being fully exploited. A virgate was equivalent to about 30 acres.

Villeins or villagers formed most of the population. The average holding was one virgate of arable land with adjoining small areas of meadow and pasture. Three classes of cottagers are mentioned: the bordars, the coscez who lived on the King's land and the cottars. At the bottom of the social scale were the serfs. A 'demesne' is land in the lord's own hands or 'home farm'.

The entries relating to Mere are:

'Land of Joscelin Riviere'
Joscelin Riviere holds Sele of the King. Almar held it at the time of King Edward and it paid geld for 2½ hides. There is land for 3 ploughs. In demesne there is 1 plough and 2 serfs and there are 5 villeins and 3 coscez with 2 ploughs. There is a mill paying 40d. and there are 3 acres of meadow. The pasture is 3 furlongs long and 3 broad. The woodland is half a league long and as much broad. It was and is worth 30s.

'Land of the King's Serjeants'
Afgeat holds Sela. In the time of King Edward it paid geld for 2½ hides. There is land for 3 ploughs. In demesne is 1 plough and there are 4 serfs and there are 8 villeins and 9 bordars with 2 ploughs. There is a mill paying 3s. and there are 4 acres of meadow and 40 acres of pasture. The woodland is half a league long and half a league broad. It is worth 30s.

Afgeat's holding has been identified with that granted in AD956 by King Eadwy to a huntsman; this, and the holding of Joscelin Riviere, equate with the two manors later known as Zeals Aylesbury (Higher Zeals) and Zeals Clevedon (Lower Zeals).

Godric the huntsman holds 1 virgate of land which pays geld in Mera. There is land for half a plough. He has there 1 coscez and half an acre of meadow. It is worth 5s.
Wulfric holds Mera. Aellic held it in the time of King Edward and it paid geld for 1½ virgate of land. There is land for half a plough which is there with 4 bordars and there is half an acre of meadow and 1 acre of pasture. It is worth 7s.6d. Wulfnoth holds 1 hide in Mere and it paid geld for so much in the time of King Edward. There is land for 1 plough which is there with 6 cottars and there are 4 acres of meadow and 1 acre of pasture. It is worth 20s.

Another manor in Mere appears as owned by the Bishop of Salisbury:

The same Bishop holds Chedelwich [now Charnage]. Algar held it in the time of King Edward and it paid geld for 5 hides. There is land for 3 ploughs. Of this land 4 hides are held in demesne and there are 2 ploughs and 5 villeins and 6 bordars and 2 coscez with 1½ ploughs. There are 10½ acres of meadow, pasture 3 furlongs long and 2 furlongs broad and woodland 2 furlongs long and 1 furlong broad. It was worth 40s., now £4. This is in exchange for 'Scepeleia'*. Hugh holds it of the Bishop.

The size of the Charnage manor described here approximates closely to that of the present Charnage Farm. Charnage was always a separate tithing of

* This holding cannot be identified.

Mere and it is likely that the holding has changed little over the centuries. A large part of the parish south of the town was designated as Woodlands tithing but this cannot be identified exactly in the Domesday record; the tithing was several times the size of what is known to have made up the land of Woodlands Manor.

Twelfth- and thirteenth-century pottery from Mere and Wilton in Salisbury Museum.

The Hundred of Mere in those days included the following tithings: Mere, Woodlands, Chadenwyche, Zeals, part of Kingston Deverill, Maiden Bradley, Stourton, West Knoyle, East Knoyle and Monkton Deverill. An entry for the Mere Hundred in the Geld Accounts in 1084 is as follows:

In the Hundred of Mere there are 86½ and 1 virgate. Of these the barons have in demesne 34 hides and half a virgate. Of these the King has 17½ hides in demesne. The Abbot of Glastonbury has 5 hides; the Abbess of Wilton has 4 hides and 1 virgate; Walter Gifard has 4 hides; Gilbert Maminot, Bishop of Lisieux, has 3½ hides and 1 virgate; and for 51 hides have been rendered to the King £15.6s. But of this money 74s. from the land of Earl William was not rendered at any term but afterwards, the four collectors of geld retained 12 pence. £3.14s. from the King's manor of Knoyle which were not rendered at any term but were afterwards rendered. Saulf moreover retained geld from 1 hide and half a virgate which he holds of Godselin de Reveria, that is 7s.6d.

The locations of these holdings can be identified: the King's 17½ hides were at East Knoyle, the Abbot of Glastonbury's 5 hides at Monkton Deverill, Walter Gifard's 4 hides at Maiden Bradley, the Abbess of Wilton's 4½ hides at West Knoyle and the Bishop of Lisieux's 4 hides at Kingston Deverill. Walein of Douai had the manor of 'Stourtone' and possibly an unidentified manor of Celdewelle. Out of the Hundred, Edward of Salisbury may have had 4 hides at Kingston Deverill or they may have been at Hill Deverill. The tithing of East Knoyle was transferred to Downton in 1330 and that of Monkton Deverill to Damerham.

In adding up the areas listed above in Domesday it seems that a large part of Mere itself escaped being recorded. It may be that, because the King was not liable to pay any form of tax, his land in Mere, kept for sporting purposes, was deliberately not included.

During medieval times it was rare for a parish the size of Mere to have had no land held by one or more of the larger religious institutions but at no time did Mere have monastic landlords. In 1130 the revenues of the church at Mere were granted by the King to Salisbury Cathedral and then appropriated by the Dean. From that time to the middle of the nineteenth century Mere was a 'Dean's Peculiar' and the Dean of Salisbury was nominally the rector of the parish. For that reason he claimed the greater tithes payable in Mere which were used for the maintenance of the cathedral. The Dean owned a number of houses in the town, mainly in the Church Street area, together with a farm of some 100 acres in scattered holdings in the open fields. This estate, as 'the Manor of the Parsonage of Mere' was leased by the Dean to the Chafin* family at the time of the Reformation and was finally sold to them by the Ecclesiastical Commissioners in 1861.

In 1227 Richard, the younger son of King John, was created Earl of Cornwall by his brother King Henry III. The earldom had been joined to the English Crown ever since the tenth century conquest of the county. Richard's son Edmund succeeded him but when Edmund died without an heir in 1280 the estate reverted to the Crown. In 1337 Edward III created his son Edward the Black Prince, then only seven years old, the first Duke of Cornwall. Thereafter, the first-born son of the monarch always became Duke of Cornwall and when there was no such heir, the property was to revert to the Crown; future monarchs were bound to surrender it on the birth of a male heir and the lands were inalienable. Only the income was available to the current Duke but it gave him independence. This arrangement continues to the present day.

In 1243 Henry III granted to Earl Richard 'the Manor of Mere with all appurtenances and that he may found there a religious house of what order he pleased'. There is no certain evidence that any monastery was ever built although Colt Hoare in his *History of Modern Wiltshire* refers to one at 'Sealys Aylesbury' (Zeals) and continues that 'there was a chapel at Zeals dedicated to St Martin, of which no trace remains'.

In 1253 Richard was given permission to build a castle in Mere. He chose to build it, quite reasonably, on the summit of the small steep hill, now known as Castle Hill, which dominates the town on its northwestern side. From a nineteenth-century excavation it has been shown that the castle was rectangular in shape, 309ft long and 102ft wide, covering the whole of the top of the hill. It had six towers, two small ones on each of the longer sides and a larger one on each of the shorter sides. It would have been built in the Norman style with thick walls, slit windows and

The spelling of the name Chafin was later changed to Chafyn.

An artist's impression of Mere Castle.

round towers. There was a hall, an outer gate, an inner gate, a deep well and a chapel. A priest was paid 50s. a year to say Mass in the chapel for the soul of the earl's second wife Sanchia Berenger. The castle officers were a constable, paid 60s.8d. a year, a warder for the day and a watchman for the night who had to share £4.11s. a year between them.

A good example of a southern English enclosure castle exists at Framlingham in Suffolk which, although larger in scale and with greater external earthwork defences, shows the kind of structure that must once have stood in Mere.

For the building of the castle Richard was given by the King 60 oak trees from his forest at Gillingham and a further ten oak trees in 1257. In 1259 *The Calendar of Close and Patent Roll* records that another 60 oak trees were given by the King for repairs to the castle in Mere. It seems extraordinary that repairs should have been necessary so soon and more repairs were done in 1300 as shown in *The Rolls of the Duchy of Cornwall* where wages paid to workmen and the prices of materials used are listed in detail.

The construction of the castle must have had a great impact on what was probably only a small farming community. It would have brought a new

prosperity to the town even when the boost given by the original building work had passed. The castle was prepared for defence – there is a reference to its having 'great stones for the engines' (engines being catapults) but it was never used in war. There was never any garrison stationed there, it was really a manorial headquarters; indeed it must have been a sizeable domestic establishment.

At the end of the thirteenth century there were two important prisoners confined at Mere Castle. During the Scottish wars of Edward I (c.1296–1305) his steward, Richard de Chiseldene, ordered that the Abbot of Scone should be taken as a rebel and traitor by the Sheriff of Wiltshire from Winchester to the Castle of Mere to be imprisoned and kept in chains. On another occasion, the Countess Margaret, estranged from her husband Edmund who became Earl of Cornwall in 1296, was forced to live in banishment in the castle and one of the towers became known thereafter as the Countess' Tower.

By the early-fourteenth century, now with its castle, Mere seems to have increased greatly in importance. The earl of that time used the manor of Mere chiefly as a stud farm and for turning out his chargers to grass. He spent much of his time at his castle at Berkhampstead to which venison was sent from Mere Park and his steward at Mere sold cheese, butter and surplus wheat and oats. In 1300 there is a record of the earl's property at Mere consisting of:

the Manor of Mere and a Castle with a farmstead and grange, cowstalls and stables; 324 acres of arable land, meadow and pasture, two parks (Conwich Park and Deverill Longwood), a fulling mill and two corn mills.

Conwich Park was situated near to the present Park Corner Farm; the name is preserved as Convish Farm

Castle Hill seen from the south.

just to the north of Park Corner, and Deverill Longwood was a woodland area, since cleared, between Whitesheet and Zeals Knoll.

The trades followed by some of the inhabitants at this time are listed as smith, carpenter, hunter, haymaker, shepherd, tanner, potter and mercer. Roger the Clerk was vicar of Mere in the year 1300 followed by Walter in 1331. In 1304–05 Mere returned two members to Parliament: Johannes Tony and Henricus de Horsington. The latter owned land between Whitehill and Gillingham Forest. In 1399 the men and tenants of the castle and lordship of Mere, being of the ancient demesne of the Crown, were confirmed as being exempt from toll throughout the whole of the kingdom.

Thomas Baker, the local historian of Mere, 1907.

By 1398 it would seem that Mere Castle was abandoned because in that year Richard II ordered lead to be stripped from its roofs for his castle at Portchester, Hampshire. When Aubrey visited the town in 1660 he was shown Castle Hill and told 'here anciently was a castle', so presumably there was no exposed stone left on the hill by then. At the end of the seventeenth century Celia Fiennes in her book *Through England on Sidesaddle at the Time of William and Mary* wrote:

By the town of Meer is a vast high hill called the Castle of Meer. It is now all grassed over and so steep that the ascent is by footsteps cut into the side of the hill. I was on the top where some had been digging and was come to a place that was arched and the walls plastered and washed white and smooth – it was but a little room. I took a piece of its walls and plaster. This shows there may be cells or vaults in the hill.

In 1798 Simpson's survey of the manor of Mere reported that:

About 50 years ago a person accidentally discovered some freestone in the foundations of the castle on the summit of the Hill and a quantity was digged out such as door cases and steps. At length an order went out from the steward to prohibit their digging out any more. Finding that there still remained a prodigious quantity of good building stone there, I caused several places to be opened, when old walls presented themselves with passages in between and several loads were thrown out with a few pieces of freestone coping and two fluted pieces that had been on the sides of a door case. The Revd Mr Grove of Mere desired to have these curious pieces and pay for them. I consented, but finding that he did not fetch them away, I immediately sent to him again, but he neglected till they were stolen. His Royal Highness's tenants thought they had a right to purchase the building stone

before strangers. I consented to this likewise but unluckily, boys (as I afterward heard) went to the top of the hill, rolled down the stones among the farmer's corn so that they could not be recovered. There is certainly a great deal of good building stone in the foundations; what freestone there may be is uncertain but it must be valuable as there is no freestone quarry within 12 miles of Mere.

Freestone is defined as sandstone or limestone that is easily cut.

In 1887 it was decided to put up a flag-pole on the top of Castle Hill to commemorate Queen Victoria's golden jubilee. In digging the hole for it some of the foundations of the castle were discovered. T.H. Baker the local historian gives the following account:

1887, June 15th. Accompanied by Mr. Wyld [Revd E.G. Wyld, vicar of Mere] to the Hill where James Fricker was digging a hole 6ft deep for the flag staff. The whole of the soil to that depth was composed of debris of the walls of the old castle, principally mortar and Mere stone but there was a piece of sheet lead about a foot square perforated with nail holes in one of which a nail remained, very little corroded [this item is now in the collection of Mere Museum]; also a large piece of freestone about 2ft long which was either a coping stone or a splayed window joint sawn off square at the ends. The stones were mostly stuck up edgeways in the same position as they fell. There were also a few bones, apparently fowl bones. On excavating a little deeper we came upon another piece of freestone, the same splay as the former piece but smaller. Both pieces were marked with a cross. We then touched what appeared to be either the drip-stone of a set-off in the castle wall or the first stones of an arch where it commenced springing. We then decided to put the flag further east and explore this hole. Below the 6ft depth we found pieces of upright wall some 10ft below this which we propose to search further on some other day. Nothing of note was found except a good stone tile perforated with a hole to nail it on. The next hole dug for the flagstaff proved to be at the exterior wall of the castle. It was faced inside with Mere stone, the middle filled with chalk. The outer face of the wall was not reached so we did not ascertain its thickness but I should say at least 2ft of it was excavated.

July 4th. Further excavation made and another wall discovered parallel with the previous one, so there is no doubt we have dug into a vaulted passage which appears to have run outside the castle walls on the south side and east of the centre. The width of the passage is 5ft. Another splayed window joint found.

The account finishes there but as the whole size and shape of the castle is known, as recorded by Frances

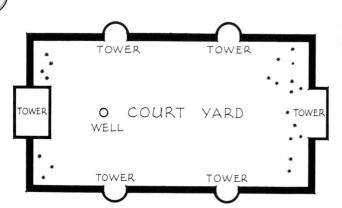

Left: *Plan of Mere Castle based on the excavations of T.H. Baker and Revd E.G. Wyld in 1887.*

Brown stoneware salt cellar found near Castle Hill.

An alabaster plaque found near Castle Hill in 1878 and now in Mere Parish Church.

The old Market House.

FROM A PAINTING BY JOHN BUCKLER, 1804.

Lovibond, Baker's daughter, in a booklet she published in 1937, further excavation must have been done. At some time a gold finger ring was found with a Latin inscription stating that it belonged to the 'Keeper of the Castle at Mere'. At the time of writing the ring's whereabouts is unknown. Two other finds were dug up at the foot of the hill and are thought to have come from the castle. One was a brown stoneware figure used as a salt cellar which is now in Salisbury Museum. It is, in fact, a seventeenth-century piece of stoneware from Germany and cannot therefore have any connection with the castle. The other find is an alabaster tablet now fixed to the north wall of the sanctuary of the Parish Church. Baker thought that this carving of the Nativity scene came from the chapel of the castle but expert opinion now dates it to 1450; it is much more likely to have come from the Parish Church when ornaments were discarded during the Reformation in 1550.

In 1408 King Henry IV granted to his son Henry, Prince of Wales, permission for him and his heirs to hold two fairs a year in Mere and he granted a charter for a market to be held on Wednesdays. The two fairs, each lasting a week, were to be held on 6 May and 24 August. The market and May fair were held regularly until the eighteenth century but there is no record of any August fair. A market cross was described as being 'ruinous and defective by default of the Vicar' in 1423. No market cross exists in Mere today. However, in medieval times a Market House was built, probably where the cross stood, in what is now The Square. It was a substantial two-storey building and in the sixteenth century was leased to William Dodington as 'a certain house or chapel called the Cross House' with shambles and shop attached. It was demolished in 1863 and replaced by the present clock tower.

There must have been a lot of building going on during the late-fourteenth and early-fifteenth centuries in Mere, which included the enlargement and rebuilding of parts of the Parish Church, the erection of Woodlands Manor in 1370–80, the provision of a house for the chantry priests in 1424, the building of a Vicarage (now The Old Rectory) and the Deanery in Castle Street, now demolished. These buildings will be described in later chapters.

The Market Place, Mere, in 1862 showing the old Market House a year before its demolition.

Chapter 4

Sixteenth-and Seventeenth-Century Mere

Although this period was one of political and religious upheaval and change, there are only scanty records of what took place in Mere at this time. That said, one well-documented local event first occurred in 1550 and was not resolved until some years after. It concerned a dispute between Lord Stourton and Mr Chafin of Zeals House over the occupancy of the demesne (home farm) lands in Mere. There was riotous behaviour and even armed conflict when the servants of one party attacked or counter-attacked the other. Eventually the matter was taken to court and Lord Stourton won the day.

In 1594 Francis Potter, son of Richard Potter, vicar of Mere, was born in the Vicarage House. He was a clever boy and studied at Trinity College, Cambridge. He was good at drawing and painting and the Founder's picture that hangs in the refectory of Trinity College was copied by him from an original one which I am unable to identify. When his father died in 1637 Francis succeeded him as rector of Kilmington where he 'led a single and monkish life without the conversation of ingenious men' until the day of his death. About 1640 he advanced the idea of curing diseases by the transfusion of blood and he invented various mechanical devices which earned him membership of the Royal Society. He wrote *An Interpretation of the Number 666* – a copy of this small book is in the collection of Mere Historical Society – which was highly regarded and translated into several languages. He died in 1678, quite blind, and was buried in the chancel of Kilmington church.

The Mere churchwardens' accounts date back as far as 1556 and, with a few missing years, continue in perfect order until 1853. The first entry in 1556 refers to profits from the Church Ale. For the church ale, two young men of the parish were chosen each year, one called the 'Cuckowe King' and his assistant the 'Prince'. They made collections from the parishioners of provisions and money to use for a Whitsuntide feast with general merrymaking. The church ale was held in the Church House and continued to be held in Mere until 1614. It was an important source of income for the church, much like the annual church fête of the present day.

The Church House stood on the land to the east of the churchyard which is now part of the garden of

1 Church Street and which had been, until 1965, a school playground. It was built in about 1580 and pulled down in 1890. A window and doorway removed from the building is incorporated into the 'Charnel House' in the south-east corner of the churchyard. This nineteenth-century building was, of course, never used as a charnel house.

The churchwardens' accounts record that a quantity of gunpowder was purchased in 1589 but sold again in 1596. It would appear that the churchwardens used the church as an arsenal for the whole of the Hundred of Mere because of the threatened invasion by Spain but when the scare was over the gunpowder was sold.

An almshouse was built in Steep Street in 1638. It contained four rooms below and four rooms above and was occupied by four families of the parish chosen by the overseers of the poor. The inmates were supported out of the rates. In about 1877 it fell into disrepair so the site and the buildings were sold by order of the Vestry for £20.

Although Mere did not feature in any of the fighting of the Civil War (1642–49), a number of happenings of that time are worth recording. Hugh Grove of Chisenbury, Wiltshire, had a son called John who married Mary, heiress of William Chafyn of Zeals House and thus John became owner of the manor of Zeals. In 1655 Hugh Grove, together with John Penruddock of Compton Chamberlayne and eight

The churchyard cross and north porch, St Michael's Parish Church, Mere.

others, proclaimed their loyalty to King Charles II at South Molton, Devon. They were all arrested by Commonwealth soldiers and imprisoned in Exeter jail. They were charged with high treason and executed. Hugh Grove was buried at Exeter where there is a memorial to him in the church of St Sydlings.

The churchyard cross in Mere was probably destroyed by Cromwellian soldiers in 1643. The fragments were later discovered by Thomas Baker as boundary markers at Mere Down and restored to the churchyard, where the incomplete cross was mounted opposite the north porch.

Dr Thomas Chafyn who was vicar of Mere from 1630–46 was roughly treated by Roundheads and died from his injuries. He had been an energetic vicar; during his time the church was paved, the south aisle re-leaded, the tower loft and churchyard walls repaired and new pews installed.

Hartgill Baron, born in 1625, was the son of a well-to-do wool merchant of Mere. He grew up to be a most daring and adroit Royalist agent, risking his life in service to Charles II during the troubled years of the Civil War and Commonwealth. It may be that he helped Charles to avoid capture during the King's perilous escape after the Battle of Worcester in 1651, for the King came in disguise to the George Inn, Mere, on 6 October for refreshment, on his way to Heale House near Salisbury. Because the Barons' business was wool merchandising which involved regular journeys to the Low Countries, Hartgill was able to be the courier for messages between the King in exile at Breda and his adherents at home. In 1660, Hartgill Baron was the first man to bring Charles the great news that Parliament had voted to invite him to return to England. He was rewarded for his services by a pension of £200 a year and given the post of

Clerk to the Privy Seal for life and made Constable of Windsor Castle. He died in 1673 and was buried in the Parish Church at Windsor where a grand memorial to him can still be seen.

In 1671 Mere seems to have suffered severely from a fire. There are no churchwardens' accounts for that year in existence but there is evidence from the registers of churches elsewhere, such as at Stanton Prior in Somerset: 'For Mere in Wiltshire, burnt, etc... August 13th, 1671. Collected 1s.6d...' and Stanton St John: '1671, collected for Mere in Wilts., 3s2d.'

By the sixteenth and seventeenth centuries the wool trade in Mere had declined to a relatively small scale. Certainly by the end of the 1800s the trade was concentrated into Devon, the Cotswolds and north-west Wiltshire. What wool spinning and weaving was done here was likely to have been for home use only. The fulling of cloth, however, was a specialised trade and we have records of several fullers in Mere at this time. The one or more fulling mills here may have served a far wider area than just the parish of Mere. A fulling mill is shown in Andrews and Drury's 1773 map of Wiltshire at the bottom of Rook Street but by the time of the 1848 Tithe Map (of which there is a copy in Mere Museum), the site is shown as just a cottage. Today, no building is visible there.

As the woollen trade diminished so the linen industry grew to become well-established in Mere. Flax was widely cultivated in the area and Mere linen weavers specialised in bed ticking, a strong twill fabric with a narrow blue band woven into the warp. Dowlas, suitable for making smocks, was also made as was cheesecloth.

James Harding, born in 1655, became a cloth and tick merchant and his son, also named James, born in 1688, continued and expanded the business. Not only

The old tithe barn in Castle Street (in right foreground), *c.1885. The barn was demolished in 1890.*

Soldiers of the Royal Field Artillery outside The Grange, Water Street, c.1908.

The garden front of The Grange, Water Street, c.1910.

Dewes House, Salisbury Street, 1948.

did he deal in ticking but he also bought and sold woollen cloth from other parts of England and traded with Hamburg, Portugal and the American colonies. He lived and worked from a house on the north side of The Square with warehousing at the back. He became a wealthy man, leaving £300,000 at his death in 1775.

Harding's business was eventually taken over by his manager, Henry Hindley, who lived and conducted his business from the house next to Harding's – the handsome double-fronted house which was to become the boardroom and offices of John Walton & Co. and in 2004 is a charity shop. Hindley's letter books covering some of his business affairs between 1762 and 1775 have survived and are in the Wiltshire Record Office at Trowbridge. He purchased raw flax and linen yarn in quite large quantities from Hamburg and from Portugal imported wine and olive oil and even small amounts of gold bullion! For importing bulky goods he used carriers to go to Newbury to collect from barges using the Thames–Kennet route from London. His exports were probably lighter loads which could be taken by carrier only. That such a substantial foreign trade should be carried on in the small and isolated country town of Mere is extraordinary and it continued until Hindley's death in 1783. Thereafter, the linen trade gradually declined in Mere and became increasingly concentrated in the industrialised areas of Scotland and Ireland.

There was, until its demolition in 1890, a building known as the Old Tithe Barn on the south side of Castle Street where, in 2004, is a car park and three adjacent houses. It was probably built earlier than the sixteenth century by the Dean of Salisbury on whose land it stood. It seems to have served the dual purpose of a residence for a bailiff at its eastern end, where there were two floors with chimney pieces at each level, and a barn at its western end for the storage of the great tithes claimed by the Dean. The stone fireplaces were saved when the building was demolished and presented by Miss Julia Chafyn Grove to Church House, Salisbury, where they are still housed in 2004.

Other sixteenth-century buildings in Mere are the George Inn and the gateway to The Chantry. The Grange, Water Street, was probably built a little earlier and was the residence of the bailiff of the Duchy of Cornwall. On its first floor there was an upper hall with two chambers and a loft and on the ground floor a large lower hall with parlour, buttery and associated rooms. In 1843 the property, as a farmhouse with extensive outbuildings, was bought by Charles Jupe, the silk throwster, who demolished all the farm buildings behind the house and used the

Dewes House, garden front, early-twentieth century.

stone to build a silk factory bordering Dark Lane. The factory has since been converted into a private house. The Grange was divided into two in 1938.

In the sixteenth and seventeenth centuries the hall of a house was the centre of all activities, since it contained the main fireplace where cooking was done, and it usually also contained most of the daytime furniture. Homestead and Barbican Cottages in Castle Street, Downlease and Dewes House in Salisbury Street are all examples of seventeenth-century houses in Mere. Dewes House was built in about 1660 with mullioned windows and a classical pedimented doorway. Until 1963 it was roofed with large stone tiles. In 1585 a Richard Dewes is listed as living in Mere so possibly the house's name derives from his family. In the eighteenth and nineteenth centuries the house was considerably enlarged on the south side with a large terrace overlooking the lawns. The garden of Dewes House was frequently used for all sorts of social occasions and indeed, many photographs taken in the nineteenth and twentieth centuries have the house and garden as a backdrop.

In 1651 the Mere Forest Charity was instituted. About 80 acres of land at Forest Deer were given in compensation for the surrender of certain rights of common which the poor of the parish had over the disafforested Forest of Gillingham. It was vested in 13 trustees for the better relieving of the poor as the trustees thought fit. The charity continues to distribute money to the needy to this day.

In the seventeenth century the economy was still a very mixed one, with many people self-sufficient. A high proportion of the properties in the town centre owned and occupied by tradesmen still had attached to them odd parcels of land in the surrounding countryside and, at one time, with rights of common grazing too, so that the blacksmith or shoemaker had his own patch of corn and a couple of pigs or sheep and a cow. Although this gradually became less common it nevertheless lasted, in some cases, until well into the nineteenth century.

Chapter 5

Eighteenth-Century Mere

Before the middle of the eighteenth century stage-coach traffic going from London to Exeter is likely to have bypassed Mere, keeping to the trackway over Mere Down. Andrews and Drury's eighteenth-century map shows a 'Hutt' at Mere Down – a transport café of its day – and we have already seen that there are milestones along the trackway dated 1750. By 1760, however, when a Wincanton Turnpike road had opened through the town, Mere was busy with stagecoach and commercial traffic and at least three of the inns had extensive stabling for horses. It has been suggested that coaches entered Mere by Old Hollow, crossed the Shreen at a ford and went up Steep Street, arriving at the inns by their back entrances. This idea is now in question because there was a perfectly good road along what is now White Road shown in a map of 1773 and the Old Hollow–Steep Street route is so narrow and twisting that coach traffic would have found it very difficult. The early stagecoach was heavy and cumbersome. It travelled at about three miles per hour over poorly maintained roads and was not fitted with springs; a light coach with springs was first made c.1750.

The following notices are from the *Salisbury Journal*:

Notice is hereby given That Edward Davis at the Angel Inn in Mere in the County of Wilts has set up a handsome new Four wheel Post Chaise and able Horses for Hire, where Gentlemen and Ladies may always depend on the best entertainment and civil usage from their most humble servant Edward Davis.
NB A Turnpike Road now runs through Mere and is the great Road from Taunton and Exeter to London and the nearest Cross Road from Blandford and Shaftesbury in Dorset to Frome and Bath in Somerset.
May 5th 1760.

Notice is hereby given That at the Ship Inn in Mere in the County of Wiltshire, Gentlemen, Ladies, Tradesmen, etc., may be supplied with a very neat Four Wheel Post Chaise with able horses and a careful driver to any part of England.

By their humble servant
John Perman.
NB A very commodious Inn for entertainments.
November 14th, 1763.

The Ship Inn (later known as the Old Ship Hotel) was originally the house of Sir John Coventry who was a Royalist in the Long Parliament. It was bought and rebuilt by Henry Andrews of Woodlands Manor in 1711 and at some time in the eighteenth century was first licensed as a coaching inn. The inn may take its name from the sailing ship badge of Johannes de Mere who founded a chantry in the church in the fourteenth century. The magnificent wrought-iron inn sign has been described as:

a gallant thing, broadening out into the middle of the road in a network of scrolls, spirals and flowering plants with a crown on top and a bunch of grapes at the end.

Old Hollow, 1968.

The old ford at the bottom of Steep Street, 1979.

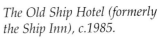

The wrought-iron sign for the Old Ship Hotel.

The Old Ship Hotel (formerly the Ship Inn), c.1985.

The White Hart Inn, on the right of the picture, c.1850.

The old fives court wall at the back of the former Angel Inn, c.1978.

It has been said that at one time there was a ship incorporated into the design but this may be pure conjecture. The sign is the work of Kingston Avery (1703–63) who was a local clock maker. An old church clock made by him still exists in the church tower but has been superseded as the main church clock by a modern one.

The Swan Inn on the north side of Salisbury Street is reputed to have been the oldest inn in Mere. In 1647 it was advertised as having stabling for 40 horses and was regularly used by drivers of road wagons. In the nineteenth century it was described as a long, low-thatched building with stabling and yards attached and with a rear access from North Street. It was demolished in 1863, having been bought by J.F. Rutter of Dewes House and houses, including Newport House opposite the Lecture Hall, were built on the site.

The White Hart Inn in The Market Place* could have been established as early as 1663. It is named in that year in the archives of the Thynne family at Longleat House but it was no longer an inn when Harding leased it in 1764. It did have a short life as an inn again between 1810 and 1860 at the end of the coaching era. In an engraving of the 1850s, possibly from a drawing by William Lander, it is shown as a large double-fronted building with an archway for coaches in the middle and a wrought-iron bracket carrying the inn sign. The inn was demolished in 1860 and two houses erected on the site, one of which is being used as a Chinese take-away in 2004.

For sports, Mere Down was a centre for hare coursing and in 1733 a horse-race took place there. It was run between the Down Farm and Whitesheet Hill and was 'patronised by all the leading gentlemen of the county' and the purse for the winner of the race was £30. Cock-fighting and bull baiting were other sports in which many indulged. In 1770 *The Salisbury and Winchester Journal* advertised:

A cock match will be fought at The Ship Inn in Mere, Wilts., to show 31 cocks of a side for 2 guineas a battle and 20 guineas each side the odd battle. To weigh, the 25th June inst. and fight the following 2 days. Burt and Osborne, Feeders.

A bullring was situated on the western side of Castle Hill and bull baiting took place there until the beginning of the nineteenth century. It is said that an old woman called 'Bull-Riding Betty' used to ride the bull to the scene of the bull fight!

The game of fives was played in Mere, as elsewhere, in the eighteenth century. The sides of church towers were used as makeshift fives courts and in the Mere churchwardens' accounts for 1705 is an item 'paid for mending the fives place window, 4 shillings'.

*What is now The Square was formerly The Market Place. It is possible that the name was changed after the Market House was demolished in 1863.

It may be that the fives court wall, which in 2004 can be seen in Angel Lane at the back of the former Angel Inn, was built at about that time, as it is recorded that the vicar and churchwardens had protested over the damage being done to their windows!

Dr Thomas Tatum, 1681–1757, practised in Mere. He had seven children and two of his sons, Thomas (born in 1712) and Harry (born in 1722) were also doctors in the town. Thomas junr is commemorated by a tablet on the wall of the north chapel in Mere Parish Church. He died in 1767 aged 55 and in his will provided for the interest on £200 to be paid to a schoolmaster for teaching poor children. This was paid until 1861. Thomas senr's fifth child, John (born in 1724), was one of the first two surgeons of the new Salisbury General Infirmary in 1766, a post he held for nine years. At the time of writing the portraits of John and his wife Catherine hang in the Postgraduate Medical Centre of Salisbury District Hospital and John's prescription book is in the collection of Salisbury Medical Society. In 1744 his sister Sarah married Nathaniel Still of Stourton, who was an apothecary at Salisbury General Infirmary, and their son, Robert, lived at Deans Orchard, Mere, where he died in 1811. He is buried in the north chapel of the Parish Church.

In Mere churchyard there is a tombstone for Edmund Dolling who died as a result of self-administered variolation – a dangerous precursor of vaccination in which smallpox serum was used rather than the milder cowpox serum used later by Jenner. The headstone reads:

*In memory of Edmund Dolling who dyed of
ye Smallpox
Which he designedly took, Sept. 6th 1737 aged
21 years.
Stop passenger, my fate deplore
Take warning by my tomb
And never like me tempt ye Lord
Least thou shouldst have my doom.*

There was a severe outbreak of smallpox in Mere in 1797 and Mr Latimer the local surgeon was paid

The tombstone of Edmund Dolling in Mere churchyard.

£37.10s. for 'vaccinating the poor'. This is surprising because Edward Jenner was still testing his vaccination theory at that time and the practice only became widespread in 1803. Thomas Latimer came to Mere in 1784 and there is a small card of that date which announces the following:

Thomas Norris, the famous tenor, born in Mere in 1742.

Mr Latimer, Surgeon, Apothecary and Man-midwife, Successor to Mr Butt, begs leave to present his respects to... and humbly solicits a continuance of ...'s favours flattering himself (that by singular diligence and attention in the execution of his abilities) to meet their future notice and esteem.

Mr Latimer was a surgeon in Mere for 50 years, dying in 1832 aged 77. There is a memorial tablet to him in St Michael's Church.

Thomas Norris, born in Mere in 1742, was the foremost tenor of his day. As a boy he was a chorister at Salisbury Cathedral and then apprenticed to the cathedral organist. He came under the patronage of James Harris, a wealthy and influential man living in The Close in Salisbury and with his help appeared several times at Drury Lane Theatre, London, singing under the direction of David Garrick. From 1761 he sang for many years at the Three Choirs Festivals and composed anthems and chants. In 1766 he was elected as organist of St John's College, Oxford, and in 1776 moved to Christ Church, Oxford. He sang in the great Handel Commemoration Concerts in Westminster Abbey and at the Salisbury Music Festivals where he was renowned for his 'pathos and dignity of expression'. He died aged only 48 and was buried at Himley, Staffordshire.

There was evidently a small brick- and tile-making industry that operated at Knowl near Barrow Street in the eighteenth and nineteenth centuries. T.H. Baker wrote that Mere Down farmhouse, where he lived, was rebuilt in about 1720 using bricks made at 'Knoll' and in the 1851 census, five tile makers are listed at 'Knowl near Barrow Street'.

An unexpected business found its way to Mere as shown by this advertisement in *The Salisbury and Winchester Journal* of 1780:

Ann Bennett, saque and mantua maker and Chamber Milliner from London, begs leave to inform the Ladies and others residing in Mere and its neighbourhood that she has taken a house in Mere where she makes all sorts of dresses in the most fashionable manner.

Those who wish to favour her with their commands may depend on having them executed in the shortest notice and on the most reasonable terms by their most obedient, humble servant Ann Bennett.

All sorts of lutestring, Holland and muslin gloves made, likewise a great Variety of child's bed linen.

Throughout the eighteenth century with its great social, industrial and political changes, the established Church had been under threat and had failed to meet the new challenges that presented themselves. A succession of Mere vicars were absentees, leaving their responsibilities to poorly paid curates. So it is not surprising that Nonconformity became a formidable rival to the Anglican Church here during the nineteenth century, as will be seen in the following chapter.

Mere Down Farmhouse, 1890.

Chapter 6

Nineteenth-Century Mere

The enclosure of land early in the nineteenth century had a great influence on the landscape we see in and around Mere today and on its inhabitants. At that time the total area of the parish which then included Zeals was 7,400 acres and of that nearly half was the subject of enclosure. It included not only common land but also a good deal of arable land worked by the smaller tenant farmers. As such, enclosure threatened the livelihood of a lot of people and not surprisingly there was great opposition to it.

In 1807 Parliament passed an Act 'for inclosing lands in the parish of Mere in the County of Wilts'. Three commissioners were appointed to implement the Act and much of the preparatory fencing off and construction of access roads was completed between 1809 and 1813. The final awards were not made until 1821. The immediate effect of enclosure was the disappearance of the little strips of arable land and the concentration of farming into larger fields by fewer farmers. The principal landowners of the district were the main beneficiaries and there was much discontent shown by the poorer people. *The Salisbury and Winchester Journal* of 19 March 1810 reported:

The inclosures of Milton and Mere Commons have excited much discontent. On Saturday se'nnight nearly 300 men from Gillingham and parts adjacent met on Maperton Hill and Pierswood and destroyed a long line of new fences. A troop of horse from Dorchester barracks is now quartered in the neighbourhood and several ringleaders of the rioters have been taken into custody. Four were lodged in Fisherton gaol where they are to remain for trial at the next assizes.

Of the accused men, ten were from Mere. They were tried in August 1810 and although found guilty, in consideration of the time they had already spent in prison, they were released and 'bound over for three years on their own recognition of £100 each.'

In spite of these troubles the somewhat premature peace rejoicings of 1814 after the abdication of Napoleon seem to have been happily celebrated, as described by *The Salisbury and Winchester Journal*:

A festival in celebration of the peace commenced at Mere on Thursday, 11th August and continued for four days.

On the first day a dinner of roast beef and plum pudding with good strong beer was served up in a large field at the foot of Castle Hill to nearly 2,000 persons. The most respectable part of the inhabitants dined in a pavilion and the poorer part was regaled at tables in front of it. In the afternoon there were rustic amusements and a dance on the green in which all classes joined. On the second day there was a grand match of singlestick which was well contested though chiefly by young players; and in the evening there was a ball at The Ship which was well attended by more than 100 respectable people of the town and neighbourhood. On Saturday the plentiful remains of Thursday's dinner were distributed amongst the poor and in the afternoon there was a match of singlestick with other amusements. On Sunday after the evening service the principal inhabitants met again in the pavilion and the ladies were regaled with tea, syllabub, etc. The whole was extremely well conducted and it is impossible that anything could exceed the harmony and happiness which prevailed during the whole four days.

In 1830 most parts of southern England were in ferment because of the high price of bread, low wages (Dorset and Wiltshire had the lowest agricultural wage in the country), employment of cheap labour from outside the country (mainly Irish workers) and the growing use of threshing machines on farms, which put more people out of work. Rioting was widespread – the so-called Swing Riots were mainly aimed at the introduction of machinery which deprived the farm-hands of their jobs. On the whole, the movement was suppressed with great harshness but in Mere the farmers seem to have capitulated completely over machines and imported labour. This result may have come about because there was an active band of Chartists in Mere at that time.

A new Poor Law was passed in 1834 setting up Unions of Parishes with Boards of Guardians to administer the provisions of the Law. Locally the Union consisted of the parishes of Mere, West Knoyle, East Knoyle, Sedgehill, Pertwood, Monkton Deverill, Kingston Deverill, Bourton, Silton, Stourton with Gasper, Kilmington and Maiden Bradley with Yarnfield. An old workhouse in Castle Street was pulled down and a new one built on the same site to

The gatehouse to the Mere Union (the workhouse), c.1925.

The Mere Union (the workhouse), Castle Street, c.1925.

the design of Gilbert Scott. The workhouse had wards for both males and females, as well as one each for boys and girls, casual wards and a sick ward. There were work areas, a yard for breaking stone and a laundry. If a man came to the workhouse, so did his family but they were accommodated separately. Inmates included the aged, paupers, bastards (sometimes with their mothers), vagrants and lunatics. Both men and women had to work for their relief. Children of the poor, when old enough, were apprenticed at the cost of the parish. The workhouse had a master and a matron and there was a teacher for the children. One of the local doctors was appointed as medical officer and the sick ward seems to have been used quite often as an accident and emergency department for the town. In 1930 a Public Assistance Act was passed, transferring the whole function of the poor law to the county councils. As a result, the Mere Union was closed down and the inmates transferred to Tisbury and elsewhere. Most of the

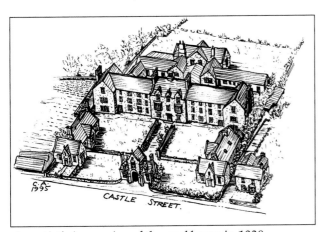

An artist's impression of the workhouse in 1930.

building has now been demolished.

During the nineteenth century quite a number of local charities gave relief to the poor but only one, the Mere Forest Charity, mentioned in Chapter 4, survives to the present day.

William Bower, by his will dated 1633, gave the one-yearly rent charge of 20s.:

... issuing out of the fourth part of two grounds of meadow and pasture called Little Lyons and Fisherhayes... to be paid after evening prayer on three days in the year (St Thomas's Day, Good Friday and Ascension Day) to five poor people of the parish, the poor of his kindred, poor housekeepers and widows with children and ashamed to beg or otherwise truly in distress being remembered before others.

Sir Hugh Wyndham, in his will dated 1680, gave the sum of 10s. paid yearly on Christmas Day to 20 of the poorest people in the parish of Mere in sums of 6d. apiece. James Harding, by his will of 1725, gave to the minister and churchwardens of Mere:

... for ever a rent charge of 50s. out of part of a farm called Benjafields at Gillingham in Dorsetshire to be distributed yearly on the Sunday next before Christmas Day by equal portions to such poor housekeepers of Mere not having any relief from the parish, as the minister and churchwardens should direct.

Robert Still, who died in 1811, bequeathed money for repairing the family vault and the remainder was to be distributed on the 1 January in every second year in sums of 2s.6d. to 'such old, decayed or infirm poor persons in Mere who were past their labour and deserving of charity.'

John Phillips of Chadenwich died in 1881, leaving £800 invested in Consols to the vicar and churchwardens of Mere, the interest on £200 for the Sunday school, the interest on £300 for blankets for the poor to be distributed on St Thomas' Day, the interest on £300 for repair of his family's tomb in the churchyard and the balance for repair of the church.

Miss Julia Chafyn Grove of Zeals House died in 1891 leaving £50 to the Dorcas Society of Mere for 'the Relief of Poor Women Lying-in and Other Cases of Need'. She also made many other bequests to local churches. A few other old charities existed during the 1800s but by the end of the nineteenth century had been lost.

By the beginning of the 1800s Nonconformity was becoming well-established in Mere. The earliest mention of Dissent here is found in the churchwardens' accounts for 1705 when a collection was made 'at ye Meeting House'. This Meeting House was at the corner of Castle Hill Lane and Manor Road but the congregation seems to have dwindled and the building was eventually demolished. The first Independent or Congregational chapel was built in 1795 by Robert Butt, a native of Mere who had prospered in a grocery and draper's business in Warminster. After a serious illness in 1790 he was restored to health and as an offering of thanks decided to build a chapel in Mere. He sold his business and bought a plot of land on the corner of Dark Lane and Boar Street for £39. At a cost of £650 he constructed a small chapel with an adjoining house for his own occupation. The chapel was dedicated on 16 November 1795 and in the following year the Revd I. Thomas was appointed as minister. On 26 October 1796, 17 people committed themselves to support the chapel. In about 1812, Butt decided to move back to Warminster and he withdrew his support. Members of the congregation and supporters raised sufficient money to repay Butt the £650 spent on the building and ownership was invested in 12 trustees. Robert Butt died in 1822 and was buried in Mere churchyard.

Charles Jupe the silk throwster mentioned in Chapter 4, like all his family, was a member of the Church of England but he married Hannah Forward, the daughter of a linen manufacturer of Zeals, whose family were ardent Congregationalists and they were both admitted to that church in Mere in 1829. He was an energetic man who spent a generous amount of time and money in the interests of Nonconformity in Mere and Zeals and, as an important employer in the town, he was no doubt influential in increasing the congregation of his adopted church. Indeed, membership grew so much that by 1852 the chapel had become too small and it was pulled down, to be replaced by another on the same site. A large schoolroom for the British School was provided under the chapel and this building still stands, having been

The first Congregational chapel built in 1795.

A SKETCH FROM MEMORY BY REVD R.P. ERLEBACH, 1852.

The second Congregational chapel, built in Boar Street in 1852.

used, after it was no longer a chapel, as the British School, the Mere Junior School, a furniture depository and now a showroom for Jeans of Salisbury Street.

In 1868 the Congregational church that is still in use in 2004 was built next to its predecessor and was funded entirely by Charles Jupe. It was much larger than the previous church – it could accommodate 600 people – but was well filled for the Sunday services at that time. The galleries were for the young people, girls on one side and boys on the other. At the time of writing the church stands virtually unaltered and is a noble example of Victorian chapel architecture. In 1874 Mr W.T. Standerwick settled £200 on trust to provide a minister's house and in 1879 the house next to the chapel – now The Old Manse – in Boar Street was bought from the Duchy of Cornwall for £300.

In 1865 a Gospel Band Barracks was opened by the Salvation Army in a building in Barton Lane on the site of the present Grove Buildings and in 1876 the Plymouth Brethren built a room on the site of the first Meeting House behind the Old Ship Hotel. Regular meetings were held there until about 1926.

Mere's Methodist church was built in 1846 of local stone in North Street and in 1859 a gallery was added

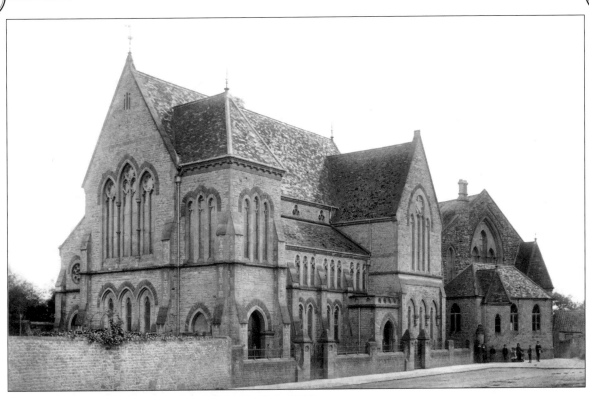

The third and present Congregational chapel built in 1868.

The interior of the Congregational chapel built in 1868.

Revd John Hyatt, minister of the Congregational Church in Mere between 1798 and 1800 (from a portrait in the Evangelical Magazine, *August, 1826).*

The Manse, Boar Street.

The Methodist church, Mere, built in 1846.

John Farley Rutter, solicitor, of Dewes House, 1890.

On the left of the picture is the Lecture Hall and next to it The Gables (formerly the Swan Coffee House) in Salisbury Street, 1997.

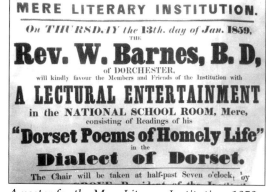

A poster for the Mere Literary Institution, 1859.

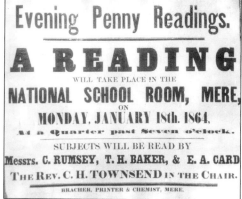

A poster for penny readings in Mere, 1864.

inside to accommodate an increasing congregation. In 1874 a schoolroom was built at the back and in 1877 new pews and windows installed in the church. Further improvements came in 1936 with a new pulpit, a communion rail, electric light and a two-manual pipe organ. During the Second World War the Methodist church (which could be 'blacked out') was used for evening services for all the Mere churches and the schoolroom used as a rest room for servicemen stationed in the town. A manse was built in 1852 next to the church and in 2004 is used as the caretaker's cottage. A new brick manse was constructed next to it in 1903 and in 1968 was converted into two flats.

In 1855 John Farley Rutter, a Quaker, bought Dewes House in Salisbury Street and set up practice there as a solicitor. There were a few other Quakers in Mere, including Edwin Bracher the chemist and printer. A Friends' Meeting House was built in 1863, incorporated into the Lecture Hall which J.F. Rutter was building in Salisbury Street at that time. The hall was used for meetings of the Mere Temperance Society and Band of Hope, concerts in aid of the British School, Methodist rallies and Liberal Party meetings (the Nonconformists were almost solid in their backing of the Liberals). Every meeting at the hall was preceded by the reading of a passage of scripture and this custom continued for some time after J.F. Rutter's death in 1899. No alcohol was permitted to be consumed on the premises.

Mere Temperance Society was formed in 1841 under the leadership of John Rutter senr, solicitor of Shaftesbury and father of J.F. Rutter. When John Farley Rutter moved to Dewes House in 1855 he became the moving spirit of the society. In 1860 a new pledge book was inaugurated with those signing it committed to abstaining 'from the use of all intoxicating drinks except under medical certificate or in a religious ordinance.' Every member was to pay a subscription of at least one penny a week, monthly tea meetings were arranged and an annual fête or seaside excursion organised. In 1870 the society expressed concern at the number of informal beer houses in the parish and this led to the closure of a number of them. In 1862 J.F. Rutter bought the Swan Inn opposite Dewes House and redeveloped the site. On part of this site Mr Rutter and Charles Jupe opened a Temperance Hall in 1865 with a large committee room on the upper floor and a reading-room below. This later became the Liberal Club and in 2004 is serves as an insurance office with Mere Snooker Club upstairs. In 1882 a 'Swan Coffee House' was opened as part of the Temperance Movement and lasted seven years. The building is now occupied by Gilyard Scarth, estate agents, and the Swan Coffee House name can still be seen on a glass panel in the inner front door. In 1874 the Society formed a successful Benefit Club providing 6s. a week sick pay for a monthly subscription of 1s. It also founded in 1876 a Mere Temperance Fife and Drum Band.

A Literary Institution was started in 1856 in Salisbury Street – its exact location is unknown – to provide a reading-room with newspapers and periodicals, and to form a library and organise lectures.

Mere Temperance Choir c.1920. Left to right, back row: *Hetty Norris, Mabel Glover, Archie Ford, Lily Taylor, D. Turner, Gladys Toogood;* fourth row: *Elsie Avery, Ethel Taylor, Evelyn Mills, Ethel Lampard, Esther Burfitt, Alan Coward, Arthur Taylor, Ellen Taylor, Ethelwyn Edmunds, Cissie Austin, Lottie Austin;* third row: *Ella Mills, Walter Ford, Kate Edmunds (choirmistress), William Burfitt, Annie Taylor, Fanny Norris;* second row: *Winifred Long, Edward Taylor, Winifred Gatehouse, Arthur Parker, Winifred Taylor, E. Turner, Edith Curtis;* front: *George Norris, Reg Ford, William Phelps, Alice Long.*

Lordsmead Mill, 1924.

Lordsmead House and Lordsmead Mill, 1924.

Below: *The Silk Houses, North Row, 1981.*

Penny readings were held, interspersed with piano and vocal solos; initially most of these events were held in the National Schoolroom with the vicar, T.H. Baker and others as readers. Later, readings were usually held in the Lecture Hall after it was built in 1863.

In 1882 a rival Church of England Temperance Society was established. It had a softer line on abstinence – there was the choice of an 'absolute' pledge or a 'moderate' one. Fortunately, the two societies seemed willing to co-operate and a joint fête was held in 1885 with a CETS Band engaged for the day. A Temperance Choir led by Henry Hooper was a feature of the Temperance Society's life and a photograph of this choir in the early-twentieth century is held by Mere Museum.

A junior section of the Mere Temperance Society called the Morning Star Band of Hope was established in 1852 and children between the ages of 5 and 16 subscribed to the pledge: 'We agree to abstain from all intoxicating drinks as beverages.' By 1890, 1,972 children had signed up and enrolments continued until 1916. The Band of Hope ceased to exist in Mere after 1939 and entries in the minute book of the Mere Temperance Society finished in 1946. Meetings of the CETS stopped during the First World War and do not seem to have been resumed.

Although the flax-spinning industry in Mere was in decline by the beginning of the nineteenth century, John Jupe took over an old grist mill at Lordsmead and converted it into Mere's first factory for the machine spinning of flax. He installed a new and more powerful water-wheel there in 1837 and this wheel survived until the Second World War. John's son, Henry, joined him and in 1838 John retired.

Henry continued as a 'Flax spinner, Linen, Tick and Cheesecloth Manufacturer' until about 1860. As the linen trade faded out a silk industry was developing in Mere to replace it. The first evidence of such a business is an advertisement in 1814 for the sale of 'a cottage and garden in Water Street with a Silk House and garden adjacent, let to Thomas Willmott, silk throwster'. The Silk House was not in Water Street; it was a building 100ft long in North Row with room for employing 120 hands and it had a plentiful supply of water. It was burnt down in 1861 and rebuilt as a row of cottages which is still standing in 2004.

In 1819 Isaiah Maggs is named as a silk throwster occupying a factory at Hinks Mill. A very large water-wheel was installed there and a substantial new building put up on the north side of the road. In the mill was living accommodation for some of the girl employees. Isaiah's son, Henry, succeeded to the business and when he died, childless, in 1840, he left his property to relatives including his nephews, Henry and Charles Jupe and Ambrose Butt. Thereafter, Charles Jupe seems to have become the dominant partner and he expanded the business to include premises in Water Street. He moved into The Grange, a former farmhouse, knocked down the farm outbuildings and built a new factory bordering Dark Lane. He also took over Lordsmead Mill where he installed woodworking machinery to produce bobbins for his silk winding. By 1851 he was employing 167 people, 151 of them women. In 1849 he took over a silk factory at Crockerton and in 1874 built yet another factory in Pound Street, Warminster. At Mere, the silk arrived unwound from the cocoons, it was cleaned, wound on to bobbins and graded.

Hinks Mill. This photo was taken before 1956.

THE BOOK OF MERE

From Mere the silk was sent to Warminster for further cleaning and sorting and then to Crockerton for spinning. Finally, it was sent elsewhere for dyeing and weaving.

Charles Jupe died in 1883 and the business was continued by his son, Isaiah, who lived at Castle House before moving to The Grange after the death of his father. Census returns show that the silk industry employed few heads of households. It was, rather, for the dependents of the breadwinners. The wage of the younger girls was as little as 2s.6d. (12½ pence in modern money) per week and for older girls, 7s. (35 pence). However, in view of the fact that the average farm worker earned 10s. (50 pence) per week, the few extra shillings, especially where three or four children were working, must have meant a lot. There were, moreover, few opportunities to earn more, other than by emigrating. In 1894 the silk factories in Mere suddenly closed down. The blame for this was placed firmly on the shoulders of foreign competition. It was a cause of great distress in the town and a number of families had members who at this time left for Canada, America and Australia. The Water Street factory reopened in 1899 employing between 20 and 30 hands for winding, drawing and doubling silk but this revival did not last. In 1906 the premises were leased to the Wilton Carpet Company for the hand weaving of carpets. The work was performed primarily by young girls who were employed at very low wages. This lasted until 1939.

In the latter part of the nineteenth century the silk industry was the largest employer of women and girls in Mere but the department store of John Walton and Co. was probably the largest employer of men and boys. John Walton came to Mere in 1864 taking over the existing draper's and grocer's business of Charles Card in The Market Place, now The Square. He had a partner, Isaiah Child, but the partnership was later dissolved and in 1868 John Walton became the sole owner. He bought neighbouring premises and transformed the business. At the height of its

John Walton, c.1900.

Duncan Walton, second son of John Walton, c.1930. He succeeded his father as director of the company.

success the company had 14 departments with branches in Maiden Bradley, Zeals, Bourton and East Knoyle. By 1895 some 75 faces appear in one group photograph of staff and in 1901 40 men were stated to be employed.

Walton's was not without competition. In 1891, one fancy goods shop, one dressmaker and milliner, two tailors, three boot and shoe shops, five bakers and seven grocers are listed in the census. In 1890 a more serious competitor arrived in the shape of the Mere and District Co-operative Society.

How was it that this small town was able to support this level of shopping facilities at that time? The economy of the area was heavily dependant upon agriculture which, in the late-nineteenth century, was having a bad time. The silk factory had closed and Walton's was the only other employer of any size. Walton's must have succeeded on the strength of its service and wide-ranging delivery provision to the scattered villages around Mere as well as to the town itself.

In about 1850 there were several carriers operating from Mere. John Knighton 'served' to Salisbury from the White Hart Inn on Mondays, Wednesdays, Thursdays and Saturdays and James Coward went to Westbury from his house in Mere every Monday and Friday. Mrs Rachel Rose went from the George Inn every Wednesday night and journeyed between Gosport and Wincanton; it is said that she regularly brought from the Wiltshire & Dorset Bank in Salisbury a box containing £300–£500 in silver to the Mere branch. During the latter part of the nineteenth century, up until the First World War, Thomas Hooper went to Frome on a Monday, to Wincanton on a Wednesday and to Warminster on a Thursday.

It was not until 1859 that the Salisbury & Yeovil Railway Company opened the line from Salisbury to Gillingham and it reached Sherborne and Yeovil the following year. The arrival of the railway must have had a great impact on the local carrier trade. A horse-bus service was started, running twice a day from Mere to Gillingham Station.

By an Act of Parliament in the

An early photograph of the staff of John Walton & Co, c.1880.

The staff of John Walton & Co., early-twentieth century.

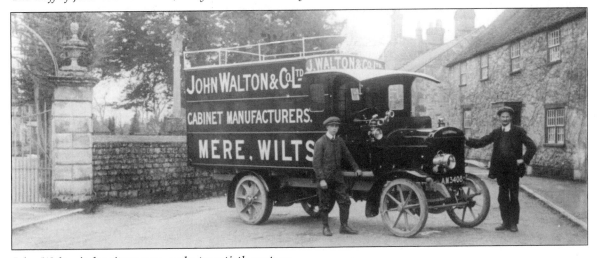

John Walton's furniture van, early-twentieth century.

Walton's ironmongery department, c.1935.

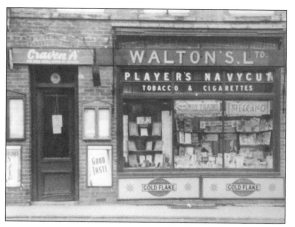

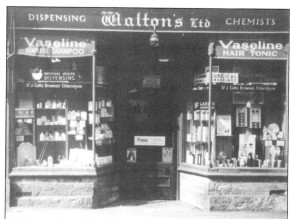

Walton's stationer's and tobacconist's department, c.1935.

Walton's pharmacy in Castle Street, c.1935.

Walton's men's outfitting and dressmaking department, c.1935.

Thomas Hooper and his carrier's van, c.1912.

Gillingham Station, 1905.

Mere's first bus, 1913.

sixteenth century each parish was required to appoint waywardens who would be responsible for the upkeep of all public roads within that parish. All cottagers and labourers were liable to do this repair work and, by a notice in the church porch, the waywardens summoned a team once a year to labour for between four and six days. This compulsory unpaid labour continued into the nineteenth century and was never very satisfactory. It was probably with great relief that the system ended in 1894 when the new Rural District Council took over responsibility. Dead Maid Quarry on the western edge of Mere was a source of road stone and continued as such until it was closed in 1930.

Three Acts of Parliament in the late-nineteenth century had a considerable effect upon Mere, as upon all other rural parishes. The Reform Act of 1884 gave the vote to agricultural labourers, the Local Government Act of 1888 set up elected county councils to take over most of the administrative work of magistrates (but Justices of the Peace were retained) and the Parish and District Councils Act of 1894 initiated a Rural District Council and Parish Council for Mere. The Guardians continued to oversee the Poor Law Unions but most of them became District Councillors with responsibility for sanitation, highways and footpaths with rights of way. So it was that in 1894 Mere and Zeals were separated into two civil parishes with their own parish councils.

As mentioned in Chapter 3, the Market House was demolished in 1863; in 1868 the present clock tower replaced it. The design of the clock tower was created by Messrs Harding and Bond of London

and it was built by the local builder Charles Coward. HRH The Prince of Wales paid for the building and his coat of arms adorns the stonework over the doorway.

In 1866 the Board of Guardians reported:

In consideration of the frequent occurrence of fever in the parish and from information received respecting the defective state of drainage, the Board strongly recommends the ratepayers to forthwith proceed with an efficient system of drainage as absolutely necessary for improving the sanitary condition of the place.

In October 1868 a public Vestry meeting discussed the problem but no action was taken. In 1871 diphtheria was common, in 1872 there was a serious outbreak of smallpox and in 1874 an epidemic of scarlet fever took hold in the town. Criticisms of the state of public health in Mere were published in the press in 1875 but it was not until 1877 that an estimate of £2,500 for installing new drainage was *Notice of a Vestry meeting, Mere, 1868.* obtained and the new system finally came into use in 1879. Even then there were complaints of frequent stoppages and it was not until piped water was installed in the town in 1909 that the problems were resolved.

A gas supply was installed in Mere as early as 1837 and the town had gas street lighting in 1839. The first gasworks were situated in North Street near the Methodist church but Miss Chafyn Grove of Zeals House complained that, in spite of having paid for gas pipes to be laid from Mere to her house, she could not get a gas supply. So the gasworks were moved to a lower part of the town at The Island, near Edgebridge. At the time of writing, gas is not produced in Mere and the gasworks site has been sold for housing. Gas is now supplied from Bournemouth.

The electric telegraph was brought to Mere in 1870 and in 1871 the first Post Office was opened in Castle Street opposite Barton Lane, moving to The Square in the 1880s.

On 21 June 1887, Queen Victoria's golden jubilee was celebrated in Mere. An organising committee had arranged for two heifers to be bought and slaughtered and the beef distributed to townsfolk in proportion to the size of their families. The Prince of Wales was asked that Castle Hill might be given to the town to mark the jubilee. He was unable to grant

The clock tower built in 1868.

Mere Post Office in 1928.

Mere fire brigade, 1895.

Mere fire brigade, 1928.

Mere fire station in The Square, c.1970, with the old fire bell.

this but arranged for it to be leased at a peppercorn rent. A flagstaff was erected on Castle Hill and John Walton donated a flag for it. Houses were decorated and a grand procession arranged. A church service was held before feasting and a bonfire on Castle Hill wound up the day's rejoicing.

As part of the jubilee celebrations a volunteer fire brigade for Mere was formed. A manual fire-engine was purchased and uniforms for the crew provided. The costs were met by public subscription. The brigade was the first of several who were summoned to Clouds House, East Knoyle, in 1889 to fight a serious fire and to Stourhead House in 1902 to fight another disastrous blaze. In 1928 the first carnival

was held in Mere, primarily to raise money for the firemen. The brigade had a horse-drawn engine and they wished to buy a redundant furniture van from Walton's to replace it. This was used for some years but was very slow. In 1938 the RDC took over responsibility and provided new equipment. The brigade gave great service during the Second World War and helped out at Bristol when the city suffered a blitz. In 1948 the unit came under the control of Wiltshire County Council. The fire-engine was at first kept in Boar Street, then in The Square and in 1972 at a new fire station in White Road where the old wrought-iron frame for the fire bell is preserved outside the station.

The diamond jubilee of Queen Victoria in 1897 was celebrated by processions, street decorations and general merrymaking and, as a lasting memorial, the approach to Castle Hill in Castle Street was laid out as a garden. In 1899 the local Conservative Club built the Victoria Hall in The Square as their contribution to the jubilee celebrations. It cost £800 and the money was raised by members who bought £5 shares. The hall was to be made available to all political parties and all sections of the community. It was the venue for Mere's first and only cinema operated by Mr Charles Jeans in the early part of the twentieth century. At the time of writing the site is occupied by a supermarket.

The nineteenth century saw great changes to the street scene, the trade, the Parish Church and the schools in Mere. These aspects will be dealt with in subsequent chapters.

Procession in Castle Street for Queen Victoria's diamond jubilee, 1897.

Procession at the western end of Castle Street for Queen Victoria's diamond jubilee, 1897.

The Victoria Hall, early-twentieth century.

The Square, c.1900.

Hazzards Hill, c.1900.

Castle Hill Approach, c.1900.

Castle Hill Approach, 1992.

The Square, c.1900.

Decorations in The Square for the visit of the Prince and Princess of Wales, 1909.

‹›

Chapter 7

Dwellings

Many of the houses in Mere are constructed from the local grey stone which is not weathering well, and with tile or slate roofs and plain windows and doorways. They are quite different from the honey-coloured stone of those in Dorset and Somerset with their mullions and embellishments often seen in villages to the west of us. Most of the houses built before the end of the nineteenth century open directly onto the street and stand one against another. As has already been said, some of the houses show evidence of the use of stone from the abandoned Mere Castle and it is significant that these often greenish stones rarely appear in houses east of the town centre.

Until well into the nineteenth century most houses were thatched and one thatched roof in The Square survived until 1910. Some of the larger houses had stone tile roofs. In 2004 the Old Ship Hotel still has its stone roof and Dewes House had one until 1963. In the days of thatched roofs, fire was a great hazard, as open fires and defective chimneys often led to disaster. In 1529 nearly all the town was burnt and in 1671 there was another serious fire that destroyed 54 houses. It is possible that some of the stone rebuilding evident in houses today may date from these times.

In the early-nineteenth century in nearby Gillingham, bricks and tiles had been made on a

Waterside, 1998.

small scale for many years but later, with the arrival of the railway, a large brickworks was established and a plentiful supply of hard red bricks became available in Mere. From about 1880 onwards, when a house was repaired or altered, the opportunity was taken to replace corners and windows and door openings with brick. A few new buildings were put up entirely of brick, such as the present pharmacy in The Square, the Duchy Cottages in Manor Road and houses in Pettridge Lane.

One area of the town, Waterside and The Fields, has a curious pattern of development: houses are jostled together in a haphazard fashion on tiny plots close to each other at odd angles and approached by the narrowest of winding footpaths. It has been suggested that these houses are the result of early 'squatting' on manorial waste ground but this is by no means certain.

With Mere's plentiful supply of water it is to be expected that a large number of houses had their own wells. To some householders today, the finding of a well on their premises comes as a surprise. Some years ago a well was found under the kitchen floor of a house in Castle Street and in 1990 a deep well was uncovered adjacent to the Talbot Garage in Salisbury Street. There used to be a town pump in Castle Street opposite Church Lane and a spring at the bottom of Old Hollow served cottages there until well into the twentieth century. There are steps down to a spring in the garden of The Chantry which supplied the house and fed the ponds.

The thatched roof of a shop in The Square (the site of Squires' fruit and flower shop in 2004).

SKETCH BY HAROLD EDMUNDS, 1910.

The Grove Buildings built in 1891.

An alley between The Fields and Waterside, 1980.

Habberley, Water Street.

DRAWING BY GERALDINE MARCHAND, 1990.

Bramley House, Castle Street, c.1980. The house was built in 1863 as a new vicarage.

Council-housing at White Road, 1980.

Prefabricated houses in Angel Lane built in the 1950s.

Castle Hill Crescent, 1980.

The nineteenth century saw the replacement of several important properties in the town centre such as the White Hart Inn and the Swan Inn and the building of a new vicarage in 1863, now Bramley House, and the Grove Buildings in 1891. Of the nineteenth century listed houses, the cottages in Church Street between The Close and Glebe House, Mere Cottage in Salisbury Street, Habberley in Water Street, and Potter's Croft in Salisbury Street are examples.

Before the First World War, six houses were put up at The Lynch by Mr Edgar Gray, builder of Mere, for Dr F.B. Rutter to help relieve the housing shortage for artisans. Also at this time 12 houses were built for the Duchy of Cornwall for tenants in various parts of Mere. In 1926 the first council-houses were completed in White Road on the eastern side of the town. Later, by 1939, 54 more council-houses were put up in Clements Lane, Barnes Place and White Road. In 1946 the RDC built six houses in Old Hollow and then in Manor Road and Denes Avenue. In these locations, German or Italian prisoners of war were drafted in as labourers. In a new venture, the council erected ten prefabricated houses in Angel Lane in the 1950s. Then, in 1958, a pleasant group of houses was designed for the council and built under Castle Hill – this became Castle Hill Crescent. A large project of 53 units including 28 bungalows and bed-sits for elderly people supervised by a resident warden, was developed at Lynch Close, Water Street, in 1970. In 1973 two-bedroomed flats were built near the recreation-ground at Queens Road.

Owner-occupied houses were built in Springfield Road in the mid-1960s and a new bridge over the River Shreen was built to provide access. In the same period, private housing went up at Lordsmead, Southbrook and Whitemarsh, where builders acquired sites and constructed access roads. A large estate of houses, flats and bungalows was built by the RDC below Castle Hill in 1975, now named Bramley Hill. This patch of housing was extended to the lower slopes of Long Hill by a good number of well-designed private homes – 'Kingsmere' – started in 1998. In 1999 a few new houses went up in Upper Water Street on land sold by North Street Nurseries. Between 2000 and 2003 the Duchy of Cornwall has built a pleasing variety of new houses on former allotments in White Road.

In spite of this apparently rapid increase in housing, the population of Mere has not increased spectacularly. In 2001 the population figure for Mere was about 2,500, much as it was in 1821. However, in 1871 it stood at 3,161 when Zeals was still included and when the greater part of Mere's population consisted of farm labourers and working men with large families. A single cottage, which today may accommodate only a couple of people, would have then housed a large family. In many cases, two such cottages have now been knocked into one. At the time of writing, four cottages typical of those originals are derelict in Shaftesbury Road. Each one had one small ground-floor room and the first floor was the same size but split into two rooms by a wooden partition – the living quarters of an entire family. Earth closet latrines were in the back garden and a well nearby supplied water. It was not until the twentieth century that local-authority housing offered those inhabiting such cottages better living conditions, releasing the old cottages for improvement by incomers to the town. The population figure fell to 1,847 in 1921 and was 2,167 in 1951. Mere is still a reasonably compact town and, we hope, will remain so.

Bramley Hill, 1980.

Lynch Close, 1974.

Houses at Kingsmere, c.1998.

New houses at White Road Gardens, 2001.

Derelict cottages in Shaftesbury Road, Mere, 2003.

The River Shreen near its source at Old Hollow.

Chapter 8

Houses of Interest

Zeals House

Zeals House was, until 1894, within the parish of Mere. It is a mansion standing in a walled park about a mile to the west of the town and its main entrance is flanked by lodges; the place is known as Black Dogs, a name that originates from the black talbot hounds that stand upon the gate pillars, the talbot dog being part of the coat of arms of the family that lived there.

The earliest record of a house on that site is dated 1304 when it was described as being 'moated about' but no moat survives now. A stone to the left of the front door is said to have on it a Saxon benchmark but the stone may have come from elsewhere rather than being a remnant of an earlier Zeals House. Matthew de Clevedon purchased the property in

The entrance to Zeals House at Black Dogs.

Zeals House, c.1990.

1372 and rebuilt the house in 1380. By the early-fifteenth century the house, together with the two manors of Zeals Aylesbury and Zeals Clevedon, had passed to the Chafyn family and it remained in the possession of their descendants until 1968. The great hall and the north wing of the present house date from the fifteenth century, the centre block was added in the seventeenth century. The final addition of the south wing and clock tower was made in 1869.

William Chafyn was Sheriff of Wiltshire in 1685 and his daughter Mary married John Grove of Chisenbury, Wiltshire, after which time the family assumed the name

Miss Julia Chafyn Grove, 1825–91.

of Chafyn Grove. Another William Chafyn was an eighteenth-century rector of Manston, Dorset, and of Wootton Rivers, Wiltshire. When challenged about holding two livings so far apart, he proved to his bishop that sermons could be preached in both churches on the same day by arranging relays of fast horses to cover the 60 miles between the two parishes! He was allowed to keep the two livings.

Legend has it that a ghost resides at Zeals House. A young woman dressed in grey is said to come down the stairs and walk out of the front door, crossing the park to the woods beyond the lake. It is believed by some to be a daughter of the house who

eloped with a servant and who was never heard of again. In 1876 a woman's skeleton was found in the woods beyond the lake, so hopes of elopement may have, in fact, ended in murder. A stone, now lost, marked the spot where the bones were found and it carried the inscription: 'A human skeleton was found here two foot deep on 22 February 1876 and re-interred in Zeals churchyard.'

Inside the house the great hall is panelled and has a high ceiling. The main drawing-room and picture gallery lead off from the southern end of the hall. Opposite the front door is a mezzanine landing giving access to a half-panelled study and library. A flagstone passage from the hall leads to the servants' quarters which includes a servants' hall. Here was once a long table on which wheeled trolleys were used for passing food from one end of the table to the other. A stone staircase has been discovered under the kitchen – eight steps down to iron-bound double doors at the foundations of the fourteenth- century building. Through the doors, two further steps lead to a vaulted cellar.

In the garden is a pretty seventeenth-century orangery, a large lake with a boat-house, and an ice house in the woods. A stone bridge spanned the south drive and led to a two-storey gazebo.

The orangery at Zeals House, c.1990.

The memorial to Julia Chafyn Grove in Mere churchyard.

The last Chafyn Grove to live at Zeals House was Miss Julia who inherited the property after the untimely death of her brother William in 1865. She died in 1891 and was the generous benefactress to many good causes mentioned in Chapter 6. The Grove Buildings are named after her. Miss Julia left her estate to her cousin, George Troyte-Bullock whose family lived in the house until 1968.

Woodlands Manor

This is a Grade I listed building set beside a quiet byroad just under a mile to the south of Mere and close to the Wiltshire/Dorset border. The present house dates from about 1370, the hall and a chapel being the oldest part. The builder of Woodlands, Thomas Dodington, was a widower who married Jane, daughter of John Guphay who held the manor at that time. Thomas was a younger son of the Dodington family of Dodington Hall, Nether Stowey, Somerset, and was descended from a Norman knight who came to England with William the Conquerer in 1066. This ancestor received large grants of land including much of Somerset and was keeper of the King's hunting forests there. The family's coat of arms features three hunting horns and for the crest, a stag with oak leaves and acorns in its mouth. The three horns on a shield are to be seen even today over the main entrance porch.

Woodlands Manor, c.1958.

Woodlands Manor in 1825.

The room below the chapel with ceiling and fireplace restored, c.1920.

The great hall, Woodlands Manor, c.1920.

Woodlands Manor when it was a farmhouse, late-nineteenth century.

The chapel is the upper part of a two-storey building. It has a barrel-vaulted roof, large windows decorated with tracery, a piscina and two arched doorways. At some time an elaborate Elizabethan-style fireplace was installed in the west end. A doorway in the north wall must have given access to an outside staircase, no longer in existence, which may have been for the use of tenants coming to the chapel. A slot in the ceiling suggests that the room was once divided into two by a wooden partition. In the nineteenth century, when the house was let to a farmer, the chapel had been used as a cheese room.

The original use of the space underneath the chapel is uncertain. It may have been simply a vault but it could have been living space for a priest. The most likely theory is that it was left open all round and used for the storage of carts. This lower storey was altered in about 1530 to convert it into a room by removing the outside stairway and putting two windows in the north wall and an inside doorway on the south side. It is now an attractive room with an ornate stone fireplace and an overmantel bearing the coat of arms of the Dodingtons impaling those of Francis: Christopher Dodington married a Margaret Francis in 1560. There is a beautiful ribbed plaster ceiling and a grape-and-vine moulded cornice around the room.

Parallel to the building just described and to the south-east of it, joined by a short passage, is a fine hall with exposed roof timbers. It is lit by one tall square-headed window (i.e. with a frame of square moulding in its upper part) with tracery and two shorter ones of a similar pattern. A magnificent medieval fireplace nine feet wide was discovered during an early-twentieth-century restoration; it was hidden behind a Victorian grate placed in cement rendering of the west wall. At some time bedrooms had been inserted at first-floor level. These were taken out in 1921 so that the full height of the hall was restored. A gallery at the eastern end of the hall is built over a screens passage leading from the entrance porch. This south porch has a small room over it with an arch-braced roof and the plaster on the wall retains an old drawing in red crayon of a horse's head. Pigeon holes were fitted round the room (probably discovered at the time when the renovations were done), which suggests that the room was once used as a dovecote.

At the eastern end of the hall, leading off the screens passage, an extension was added with a massive fireplace, probably in the fifteenth century, to provide a kitchen block. From the middle of this eastern side of the house a garden door leads, via a stone-flagged path, to a gate on the road. Near the door is a deep well and when it was cleaned out some years ago, pewter spoons, an Elizabethan jug, seventeenth-century knives and forks and a small pewter measure were found.

The Dodington family seems to have fallen on hard times, probably as a result of the Civil War and in 1705 the house and its 300-acre estate was acquired by Sir Matthew Andrews, a successful London merchant. By the mid-eighteenth century the whole estate was let as a farm. The house became just a farmhouse, was neglected by absentee landlords and became very dilapidated. In 1887 a scheme of repairs was prepared in which some of the stone windows were to be replaced by modern ones, the chapel roof

Woodlands Manor, c.1920.

Above: *The Chantry, early-twentieth century.*

Right: *The Chantry, 1987.*

Below: *Deans Orchard, c.1998.*

boarded over and the plaster ceiling in the room below the chapel taken down. Fortunately, this scheme was stopped and a careful programme of restoration took place in its stead. In 1918 Mr Meyrick Jones, the new owner, undertook further extensive renovation lasting three or four years. He found the room below the chapel had been used as a kitchen and the beautiful ceiling was badly stained by smoke. The Elizabethan fireplace was carefully removed, cleaned and repaired. A blocked-up door in the north wall was opened and the door in the south wall replaced with a Tudor one, fitted with a splendid old lock made in Mere. He undertook the extensive restoration of the hall and improved the kitchen wing, adding a bedroom to the south-east corner using sixteenth-century panelling to furnish it.

In 1949–50 the then owner, Mr Leigh Holman, undertook the building of a new wing adjoining the west end of the hall, using stone from an old cottage demolished at Donhead. He fitted it out with old oak doors and new latches and hinges specially made by a Mere blacksmith. The new work has blended in perfectly with the old. The gardens had been laid out by Mr Meyrick Jones and subsequent owners have added to them, making a fine setting for this lovely old house. The owners at the time of writing, Mr and Mrs Louis Stanton, have continued with careful restoration and improvements.

The Chantry

In 1424, Henry VI allowed the Dean and Chapter of Salisbury to give the chaplains of the Chantry of the Blessed Virgin Mary in the church of Mere 'a certain piece of their garden on the south side of the church of about one acre for the building of a house suitable for the common use of the aforesaid chaplains.' This gives us a likely date for the origins of the house. Three chantry priests were to be accommodated and there were priests living in the house until 1548 when, because all chantry endowments had been taken over by the Crown in 1546, the property was granted to Sir John Thynne. He rented it out and then sold it in 1563 to Thomas Chafyn. In order to turn what had been an institutional building into a family home, major internal alterations were made. For example, high-ceilinged rooms had extra floors put in, which were removed at a much later date with the result that in the great hall a fireplace can still be seen high up on the wall. Dormer windows were inserted to light a new upper room in the roof, as shown in a nineteenth-century painting. Spiral staircases were probably removed then as well, for there are tiny windows, now restored, which must have once lit stairways.

In 1635 the house is described as having:

a Hall, Parlour Chamber, Little Parlour, Kitchen, Cock Loft, Little Chamber, Porch on the north side, Porch on the south side, Little Buttery, Stable and Back Syde fenced with posts and rails and garden fenced with stone walls.

Large rectangular windows on the north side and a large chimney in the kitchen probably date from this time.

Over the years as the house changed from home to school several times over, rooms were partitioned, passages added, early windows blocked and new ones opened. The beautiful stone shell became hidden under plaster, timber dados and cast-iron grates. The fine timber roof was concealed under bedroom ceilings of lath and plaster. Fortunately, the exterior was left largely untouched. The Chantry is famous for having housed the school of William Barnes, the Dorset dialect poet, from 1827 to 1835 and some of his poems were written there.

A major renovation of the house was undertaken when it was purchased by Mr and Mrs Frank Newby in the 1960s. The hall was restored to its full height and its fine timbered roof uncovered. Most of the medieval windows were reopened and most ground-floor rooms could then be lit from both south and north except in the hall, but even there, traces of a very large window on the north wall were evident. Old Chilmark stone from derelict cottages, ancient timbers, large stone slabs from Tisbury, weathered elm planks from Gillingham and specially made windows forged by a Mere blacksmith were used.

During some earlier twentieth-century repair work, a floor was taken up in one of the downstairs rooms and bones were discovered. They proved to be those of a man, a woman and a dog and were several centuries old. Nothing is known of how they got there and the human bones were reburied in the churchyard.

In 1969 a portion of the garden of neighbouring Deans Orchard, including a large pond fed by a spring, was sold to the owners of The Chantry. By the side of the pond is some old masonry that might indicate the site of a corn-mill which is known to have existed thereabouts in 1280. The garden, now with its two ponds and a waterfall, adds considerably to the charm of this historic house. At the time of writing The Chantry is the home of Mr and Mrs Philip Coward.

Deans Orchard

This house on the south side of the churchyard was built in 1708 on land that had been granted to the Dean and Chapter of Salisbury in the late-thirteenth century. This land had been described as follows:

one garden and small croft with their belongings and also a mill for grinding corn in the ville of Mere... which said garden and croft lie adjacent to the house of the Dean on the south side.

Above: *The garden front of The Grange, Water Street, in the early-twentieth century.*

Right: *Dewes House, Salisbury Street, c.1956.*

The doctors' surgery in the corner of the town car park, 1990.

It was known as Mere Garden until the sixteenth century. It became known as Deans Orchard in the following century.

In 1751 the house was enlarged by the addition of a spacious drawing-room with a high ceiling and wide fireplace and bedrooms above. An extension was added at some time to its north side and, curiously, the original front door with its letter-box and north-facing windows that had looked out on to the churchyard have been retained in the hall passageway. The windows now serve as display cabinets. In the early-twentieth century a small undistinguished wing was added to the western end of the house to provide kitchen accommodation.

In 1754 the property was leased to Thomas Tatum the local doctor. After his death in 1767 the lease was transferred to his sister, Sarah Still, wife of Nathaniel Still the apothecary. Deans Orchard remained in the occupation of the Still family until the early-nineteenth century and many members of the family are buried in the north chapel of Mere Parish Church. Various tenants followed the Stills and then in 1943 when the vicarage in Castle Street (now Bramley House) became too large and expensive to maintain, Deans Orchard was chosen to be the vicarage and remained so until 1969 when a modern house was built on a field behind it for the vicar. Deans Orchard was sold by the Ecclesiastical Commissioners to Mr John Flanaghan and soon after his death in 1973 it was bought by Dr and Mrs Michael Plaxton.

The Grange

This house in Water Street was owned by the Duchy of Cornwall until 1896 and is thought to have been at one time the residence of the bailiff to the Duchy. It probably dates from the second half of the fifteenth century and is a Grade II listed building. The Grange was advertised in 1774 as 'a large and commodious farmhouse with convenient outbuildings'. These outbuildings, with the house, formed a four-sided farmyard. The tenant farmer leaving in 1774 was a William Wickham and it was another William Wickham who, on retiring from farming, put his livestock up for sale there in 1843. The next occupier was Charles Jupe the silk throwster. He demolished the farm outbuildings to make way for his silk factory. In about 1910, Duncan Walton of John Walton & Co. lived in the house until his death in 1943. In 1938, after the death of Mrs Walton, the house was divided into two, one for Mr Walton and the other for one of his daughters. At the time of writing 1, The Grange is occupied by Mr Christopher Richards the artist and bookseller and 2, The Grange by Mrs Hilary Willoughby.

Dewes House

This handsome house in Salisbury Street was built in about 1660. It has a well-proportioned symmetrical front with mullioned windows and a classical pedimented doorway. It was advertised for letting in 1795 in *The Salisbury and Winchester Journal*:

1795, Mere, Wilts. To be let or rented immediately. An exceedingly convenient Family House in good repair consisting of an entrance hall floored with oak, two parlours well furnished with handsome chimney pieces, two large cellars with wine vaults, fine bed chambers with dressing rooms, three garrets, kitchen, brewhouse and all other requisites; stabling for four horses, coach house and other buildings, a piece of land adjoining containing two acres exceedingly rich, now used as garden ground partly walled in and planted with fruit trees. Part of the buildings have been recently erected and the whole cost about £1,500 in building.

In the nineteenth century the house was considerably enlarged by the addition of rooms on the south side looking out on extensive lawns. Between 1855 and 1926 Dewes House was the home of the Rutter family, solicitors and doctors. The garden was the venue for many social occasions during their time and long after; church fêtes were regularly held in the Lecture Hall and Dewes House garden until the 1970s.

In the 1960s the eastern end of the house was divided off to form two smaller houses, Dewes Lodge and Courtyard Cottage and beyond that, more of the property was sold and converted into what are now 1–3 Wyvern House. Also around this time, with the demolishing of a house and use of garden land behind it, a town car park was made. In 1989/90 a piece of land in the south-east corner of the car park where a Ranger Guides' Hut stood and which once belonged to Dewes House, was sold by the Lecture Hall Trust to the local doctors for a new surgery.

Glebe House

This house in Church Street was formerly called Parsonage Farm and the present house is likely to have been the one described in 1771 as a 'new or newly tiled house called Dewdneys' opposite the churchyard. It seems that Farmer Dewdney (probably Aaron Dewdney who was churchwarden in 1773)

An early-twentieth-century photo of Glebe House, Church Street, formerly Parsonage Farm.

59

gave up his tenancy in 1771 and was followed by a Maidment and many others until 1861 when it was sold by the Ecclesiastical Commissioners to the Chafyn Groves of Zeals House. Some years later they sold the house with a small piece of land as a garden to Edwin Card, the Mere bank manager, for £510. In 1904 Edward Angrave bought it and ran a preparatory school for boys there. In 1927 he sold the property to Mr F.A. Coward and his grandson continues there. In 2004 it is once more a school – Stourbridge House – with Mrs Elisabeth Coward as headmistress.

The Old Rectory

This former vicarage (it was never a rectory) stands to the west of Mere Parish Church. In 1774 on the death of the Revd Caleb Perfect, the Revd Thomas Staples succeeded him but died within a year. Either before or soon after his death, the house was burnt down and his widow was compelled to rebuild it. As such, most of the present house dates from that period but there are two rooms remaining of the earlier house where a large kitchen fireplace, old casement windows and an arch leading to the back of the house can still be seen.

In 1863, Henry Townsend, vicar at that time, petitioned that the house should be sold as it was 'in a most dilapidated state'. A large and imposing new vicarage was built below Long Hill (now Bramley House) in 1865. The old vicarage, renamed Layfield House, was sold to William Mitchell, a member of an old farming family of Mere. He lived there until his death in 1889 when it was bought by William Wiltshire. He died four years later and his widow married John Hartgill, the son of the brewer at Zeals. In 1912 John Hartgill's son by his first marriage occupied the house. In 1935 it was bought by Col C.H. Walsh who renamed it The Old Rectory. In 1964, author Dr Longbourne bought it, converting the coach-house into a surgery which was in use until shortly before his retirement in 1990. The property remains in his family in 2004.

St Ann's

This property stands at the corner of Church Street and Church Lane, opposite the north-west corner of the churchyard. It was originally two seventeenth-century cottages but has had late-nineteenth-century additions at the back. One cottage was occupied by James Cross the sexton and then by his son Frederick who died in 1881. On his widow's death the two cottages were probably then made into one house where the Revd William Chell, the curate, lived.

The Old Rectory, Church Street, 1969.

Church Street, looking towards St Ann's, c.1948.

After his death in 1920 his unmarried sister lived there and for a short time had a school there. From 1947 until 1961 Dr Owen Hart and his family occupied the house, from where he ran his surgery. The house is now the home of Lady Ebbisham.

The Old House

The Old House is at the beginning of Church Street, on the corner of Angel Lane. A stone on the corner bears the date 1720. It has two front doors, the second of which is most likely to have been used as a surgery entrance when it was Dr Rumsey's house between 1845 and 1877. In 1784 it was advertised for sale in *The Salisbury and Winchester Journal* as follows:

To the Faculty, 1784.
To be lett and entered upon on or before Michaelmas next. A large and convenient Dwelling House in exceeding good repair with a neat and well accustomed Apothecary's Shop situated near the Market Place of Mere, Wilts., now in the occupation of the proprietor, Mr. J.S. Butt. The dwelling house consists of a good parlour, 16ft by 20ft, a hall, the shop, a pantry, kitchen, brewhouse, six bedchambers and garrets over them, a good underground cellar, a stable for two horses, coach house and two walled gardens; also half an acre of meadow ground near the house. For particulars, enquire of Mr. J.S. Butt, surgeon, who is removing to London and is inclined to dispose of his business in favour of any Gentleman of the Faculty who will enter on the above premises and take the shell of the shop and remaining part of the stock in trade at valuation.

It is apparent that James Butt did not go to London but retired and continued living in Mere, perhaps in part of his old house, for he died in 1807 aged 88 having fallen out of one of the windows there. He has a memorial plaque in Mere Parish Church.

By the end of the nineteenth century a coach-house and garden on the opposite side of the road (occupied by The Borogrove in 2004) was added to the property. Mr Duncan Walton lived in the house from about 1903–10. In the 1950s it was the Tudor Tea Rooms, a business transferred there from the rear of

The Old House, Church Street, when it was the Tudor Tea Rooms, c.1950.

The garden front of The Old House, Church Street, early-twentieth century.

the old Tudor house in Salisbury Street. The tea shop was taken over by Miss Sylvia Whyte and in 1962 she offered it as a meeting place for a newly formed old people's club. The club assumed the name 'White Tudor Club' in her honour and continues to meet each Wednesday afternoon but now in the Grove Buildings. After Miss Whyte retired the property became known as the Pestle and Mortar restaurant in the ownership of Mr and Mrs Anderson and then in 1986 the present owners, Brigadier and Mrs Webster, made it their home.

Charnage

Charnage Farmhouse lies about a mile east from the centre of Mere. Charnage was a tithing mentioned in Domesday as a manor of the Bishop of Salisbury and named Chedelwick ('house in a wood'). It was later known as Chadenwyche before it finally became

Charnage Farmhouse, east front, 1980.

Charnage Farmhouse, west front, 1998.

Lower Mere Park Farmhouse, 1979.

Charnage. It once possessed a chapel dedicated to St Martin of which a fragment of a wall remains in the present kitchen garden. In the fourteenth century it belonged to Sir John Bettesthorne whose memorial brass is in Mere Parish Church.

In 1576 the farm was bought by Thomas Aubrey of Reading. It was sold to Sir Thomas Coventry in 1639, before being sold to the Wyndhams. Some time in the eighteenth century it came into the ownership of the Hoares of Stourhead. In 1780 the Phillips family became tenants and it remained with them until the 1870s when William White took it over. In 1891 the house and farm were bought from Sir Henry Hoare for Arthur White, on his marriage, by his father and father-in-law. It has remained in that family ever since, the present occupiers being Mr and Mrs John White.

Mere Park

This was an ancient royal deer park and it covers about a square mile in the southernmost part of the parish. At its southern boundary is a 'Saxon mark' – a ditch, a hedge and a raised mound on each side of the ditch which is 22 yards wide and half a mile long. To the south of this boundary was the Forest of Gillingham and it is here that the counties of Wiltshire and Dorset meet. In the south-west corner of the park is a deep pond which is thought to have originally supplied fish to royalty at King's Court, Gillingham, and Mere Castle.

Among several distinguished stewards of the park were Sir Walter Raleigh and his brother Carew. Carew was MP for Downton near Salisbury and was able to devote more time to the office than did his famous brother. At the end of the nineteenth century a fine jewelled dress sword was found in the fish pond. It was identified at the British Museum as having probably belonged to Sir Walter Raleigh. Unfortunately, at the time of writing its location is no longer known.

There are two farmhouses within the present Mere Park. At Lower Mere Park the house is part sixteenth century with additions made in 1726 and again in 1884. In 1822 a survey reported that at Upper Mere Park the house was very ancient and once had a moat around it but it was considered to be past repair. It was consequently demolished and the existing house built. From 1844 to 2004 all the tenant farmers at Mere Park have been from the Mitchell family.

Castle House

This house stood at the eastern end of the town at the top of Old Hollow. It was built by Charles Jupe in 1860 for his son Isaiah. It was of a very pleasing design with the front walls built in stone in a style known as 'snailcreep'. It was the home of the Revd Ernest Borradaile at the end of the nineteenth century who was founder and chairman of the Mere and District Conservative Club. He was foremost in getting the Victoria Hall built in 1899 but, sadly, died in the following year. For some years Mrs Gladys Matthews lived in Castle House. In the 1950s and 1960s it was used as a children's home run by the County Council. It was demolished when Mere bypass was built in 1975.

Higher Mere Park Farm, 1979.

Castle House, c.1925.

Chapter 9

Churches

The Parish Church

A church dedicated to St Michael the Archangel probably existed on the site of the present building before the Norman Conquest. The Register of Bishop Osmund, 1091, states that William the Conquerer granted revenues of the church at Mere to the bishop and Bishop Osmund used half of this money to help pay for building a cathedral at Old Sarum.

It is probable that the rough masonry wall at the western end of the nave dates from this eleventh-century church. In the fifteenth century the present arch was put into this wall and the line of the roof of the original church can be seen above this arch. When William Wanda, Dean of Salisbury, visited the church in 1220 he found an incomplete building with three altars, a tower and bells but no roof on the chancel. Presumably there was a major rebuilding of the church at that time.

Surviving thirteenth-century work in the chancel is a recess on the north side of the altar – probably an

Easter sepulchre – and a piscina (the westernmost of two) on the south side of the altar and a doorway in the north wall of the sanctuary. This doorway probably led into a sacristy; there is a piscina eastwards of the door. Before the end of the thirteenth century the sacristy was demolished and the use of the doorway ceased. A window was then inserted above it, the sill of which cut across the top of the disused door. The sill was raised when the doorway came back into use, possibly in quite recent times.

A north chapel, now called the Still chapel, was founded in about 1350 most probably by the Stourton family. At first it extended eastwards only as far as the window described above but soon afterwards it was enlarged towards the east and widened. The stone used was the greenish sandstone from Wolverton mixed with Chilmark stone. The chapel is likely to have been associated with the royal manor of Mere; William Stourton was steward of the Principality of Wales and, significantly, of the Duchy of Cornwall too. There is certainly a Stourton connection with the chapel for on the balcony at its western end which faces into the north aisle are seven tracery panels bearing coats of arms, 16 in all, which relate to the various alliances of the Stourton family. In the seventeenth century one of the Baron family was bailiff of the manor of Mere and several of that family are buried in the chapel. Some of the lands that had endowed the chantry were later in the hands of the Andrews family, a few of whom were buried in the vault under the chapel floor before the Stills of Deans Orchard appropriated it.

The roof of the north chapel is a wagon-head vault divided into 20 plastered panels by oak ribs. It has some old carved bosses at the intersections and also a good shield bearing the date 1604. There is also a shield of poorer quality dated 1791, in which year the chapel was ceiled and whitewashed, Robert Still contributing to the cost. A hatchment of the Still family impaling the arms of Skrine hangs on the chapel wall. To the left of the door leading into the chancel is a small remnant of a piece of chain for a chained bible. In the nineteenth century the chapel was furnished with cheap seating 'for the poor'.

To the south of the chancel is another chantry chapel built by John of Mere, steward of the manor

St Michael the Archangel Church, 1996.

The coats of arms on the balcony in the north aisle of St Michael's Church.

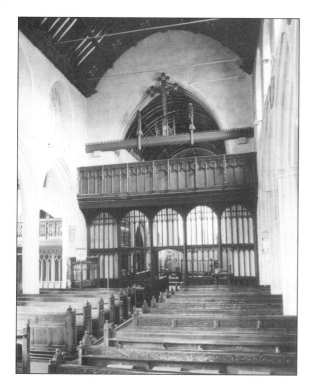

Interior of St Michael's Church, 1990.

Fourteenth-century glass in a window of the Bettesthorne chantry chapel, St Michael's Church, showing St Martin dividing his cloak with a beggar.

The fifteenth-century chancel screen in St Michael's Church.

The brass of Sir John Bettesthorne in St Michael's Church.

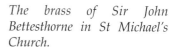

An angel corbel in the roof of St Michael's Church.

PHOTOGRAPH BY DEREK WILSON, 1997.

under King Edward II. He founded it in 1325 so that Mass might be said for the soul of Queen Margaret, the second wife of Edward I, as well as for the souls of himself and his wife. Its patronage passed from John of Mere to Roger Bettesthorne and then, through the marriage of his great-granddaughter, to the Berkeley family. Through another marriage, it passed to the Comptons with whom it remained until the Reformation in the sixteenth century. After the Reformation it passed to the Chafyn and Grove families.

Centrally in the floor of the south chapel lies the brass of Sir John Bettesthorne. It is one of only 11 known in the country showing a dominical letter by which the days of the week are calculated and by which the day of his death is therefore known. Close to the south side of the altar is a broken brass of about 1430. It is probably for John Berkeley who married Elizabeth Bettesthorne, heiress of John Bettesthorne. Their son, Maurice, was said to be the slayer of the Bisterne (near Ringwood) Dragon and at the top of the south-east window is Maurice's coat of arms. Antiquarian John Aubrey recorded a series of coats of arms that were displayed in the windows of this chapel in the seventeenth century (but Maurice's was not mentioned). This surviving coat of arms was removed to Zeals House in 1865 but returned in 1895. In the top lights of the westernmost window are four panels which date back to the fourteenth century, depicting St Nicholas, St Martin, St Christopher and an unidentified pope. Seventeenth-century funerary armour and hatchments of the Chafyn and Grove families hang on the walls. At the sanctuary step are fragments of fourteenth-century tiles. Between the chapel and the chancel is a Purbeck marble tomb. It may be that of John, 1st Lord Stourton who died in 1463 but it is more likely to be that of his grandson, the 3rd Lord, who married a Berkeley, the family who had the chantry at that time. He died in 1485.

In about 1380, because the north chapel had been widened and the south chapel built, both north and south aisles of the church were out of line with the outer walls of the chapels and had to be rebuilt, increasing the aisle widths by more than four feet. North and south porches were built at this time with a room over each. The north porch has a fine deco-rated period vault and outside it, in a niche over the doorway, is a statue of the Archangel Michael slaying a dragon. The statue is older than the porch, contem-porary with the twelfth-century Romanesque sculp-ture seen at Malmesbury Abbey. A holy-water stoop to the left of the doorway suggests that the saint was an object of veneration. Inside the porch is another niche over the inner door that in 2004 houses an unidentified headless statue found in a nearby pond. Outside, on a turret staircase, are two unusual carv-ings of bats. The room over this porch, called the 'Treasurye Lofte' in 1636, was used for meetings of the Vestry and later for a church museum. The room

over the south porch was a priest's chamber and has a little window as a 'peep' into the church. The south porch was rebuilt in 1707 and a new south window for the upper room put in during the late-nineteenth or early-twentieth century.

In the later part of the fifteenth century the church was extensively remodelled. The chancel arch and its roof were raised, the east window replaced, the north and south arcades of the nave rebuilt, a clerestory added and a higher nave roof laid. The tower was heightened and a new rood-screen made. On the north side of the nave are 'blind' windows which match those of the clerestory on the south side; these were put in after the north aisle roof was raised. This left the church much as it is today.

During the reigns of King Edward VI (1547–53) and Queen Elizabeth I (1558–1603) much destruction was done to ornaments and furnishings in the church. The rood and the panels fronting the rood-loft over the screen were removed. The discarded items might have included the fifteenth-century alabaster plaque now affixed to the north wall of the sanctuary which was mentioned in Chapter 3. After it was found in a garden at the foot of Castle Hill in 1878 it was taken to a lady in Mere who collected antiques. It was later bought from her by T.H. Baker for 10s., although after his death it was

The north porch of St Michael's Church with a twelfth-century statue of the Archangel Michael above the doorway. DRAWING BY GERALDINE MARCHAND, 1990.

presented to the church by his daughter as a memorial to her father.

Over the doorway leading out of the church into the north porch are the royal arms which originally hung over the chancel arch. They are of particular interest not only because they are the arms of James II, which are rare, but because they are the earliest of his reign in any church.

The beautiful fifteenth-century rood-screen has areas above the coving showing traces of original colouring; the whole screen bore colour until 1856 when restorations were performed. In 1815 the rood-loft, referred to as 'the middle gallery' was filled with 36 seats 'to be reserved for a school'. There is a blocked doorway in the present vestry, part of the north chapel, that once gave access to the rood-loft but by 1815 access would have been by the north aisle gallery. In 1898 a rood-beam supporting a cross and two figures was installed above the screen. The cross carried no figure of Christ because of strong local prejudice against 'Romanish practices', so the figures of St John and Our Lady were left gazing at an empty cross until 1914 when the Christ figure was added as a memorial to the Revd J. Lloyd.

In the seventeenth century there was a gallery at the east end of the north aisle to accommodate nine people. A gallery of a similar size was put into the east end of the south aisle in 1704. Another gallery at the west end of the nave under the tower was made in 1705 to accommodate 24 singers and an organ. All the galleries were cleared away in 1855/56.

The choir stalls are a mixture of old and new; there are fifteenth-century panels in the fronts of the forward stalls and these stalls have on their western ends the arms of Troyte and Chafyn Grove carved in the early-twentieth century. The back stalls have the arms of Gilbert Kymer on their bench ends and are fifteenth century in origin. Gilbert Kymer was a distinguished Dean of Salisbury and Mere's rector between 1449 and 1463. He was physician to King Henry VI and Chancellor of Oxford University. The back stalls also have fine misericords, those on the south genuinely dating to the fifteenth century and those on the north side dating to the twentieth.

The pews in the nave are good, made by 'William Walter the Joyner' of Maiden Bradley in 1640, costing £86.11s.10d. They are furnished with honey-coloured hassocks worked in a variety of designs by parishioners between the 1970s and 2000. In 1712 the wall between the nave and the south aisle had become unsafe and was rebuilt and a new nave roof put on. In 1856 the nave roof was restored again and in 1998 the ceiling panels were added. All the roof bosses are nineteenth-century work but the angels on the wall plates bearing symbols of the Passion were made at the time of the rebuilding of the south wall in 1712. The ceiling over the lower stage of the tower is probably fifteenth century in origin; it is richly panelled and has tracery but has been much restored. Before 1856 the pulpit was on the south side of the nave. In that year it was rebuilt on the north side, using various pieces of old oak which may have included the old pulpit and its fittings. Further alterations to the pulpit were made in 1895 when panels were removed from it and restored to the north aisle gallery. There is a record of a medieval pulpit being replaced in 1625 by one 'with a peg for the preacher's hat'.

A Congregational choir outing in Matthew Norris' wagonette, c.1910.

Bells ready for rehanging, St Michael's Church, 1911.

The tower of St Michael's Church after lightning damage to the south-west pinnacle in 1977.

The '12 apostles', yew trees, in the north-west corner of the churchyard, c.1992.

The font in the south aisle has a bowl which is late-fifteenth-century work in Purbeck marble; it is octagonal, each side having a quatrefoil and a plain shield in the centre. The font stem and base were renewed in 1855 and again in 1895. The font was originally located under the tower. In the south aisle near the font there is a thirteenth-century niche and a piscina below it which must have been retained when the south wall was rebuilt and which were discovered behind plaster in the early-twentieth century. Behind the font is an engraved window of 1983 by John Finnie depicting the induction of the Revd Ben Elliott to the parish in 1981. The best Victorian stained-glass windows in the church are at the west ends of the aisles. They are by Henry Holiday in a style similar to that of Burne-Jones.

There is a sanctus bell cote at the eastern end of the nave roof. The bell was rung from the north chapel under the organ loft; there is a 'squint' in one of the mullions of the oak screen there, through which the server in charge of the bell (who was also organ blower) could see the priest at the altar and so was able to ring the bell at the right moments during a service. The bell was lost for most of the nineteenth century but in 1895 was rediscovered in the cellar of Deans Orchard and reclaimed for the bell cote.

The church tower is very fine. It is 125ft high to the top of its pinnacles and divided into three stages by string courses. At each corner is an octagonal buttress; the buttress on the north-west corner contains a staircase to the roof. The middle stage is divided into two,

the clock chamber is above and the ringing chamber below. In the clock chamber is a disused eighteenth-century clock. A new clock and chimes were installed as a Second World War memorial and a clock dial was put on the eastern face of the tower in 1948. In the top stage of the tower are eight bells, the oldest of which dates from the fifteenth century. In 1911 the bells were rehung in a steel frame, replacing old oak beams which were later turned into furniture in John Walton's workshops. Two new bells were added at this time and an original bell recast. In 1991 the bells were rehung on ball bearings and various new fittings made. Mere is a popular venue for visiting bell-ringers. The tower pinnacles have needed repair many times since 1568. In 1888 the north-east pinnacle was decayed and completely rebuilt. The north-west pinnacle was struck by lightning in 1878 and the south-west pinnacle struck by lightning in 1974 and again, with more severe damage, in 1977. The weather-vanes on the pinnacles were gilded in 1982.

A yew tree was planted in the churchyard in 1636 and another, presumably the present one, in 1707. In 1732 30 lime trees were planted beside the churchyard path and another ten in 1892. In the late 1970s 14 new lime trees were donated by Mr Jack Paul as replacements. The main gates and gate piers were erected in 1716 at a cost of £11. The churchyard was closed for burials in 1856 when a new cemetery was made in Angel Lane. In 1882 the churchyard was levelled and planted with flower-beds and the '12 apostles' yew trees lining the path in the north-west corner may

The gateway to the churchyard, St Michael's Church, 1995.

Mere Parish Church choir and clergy, c.1910; the Revd Francis Trotman, vicar, is sitting right of centre.

The induction of Revd John Smith as vicar of Mere, West Knoyle and Maiden Bradley by the Bishop of Salisbury, 1976. Left to right: Mrs Higgins (churchwarden of Maiden Bradley), Mr Emblin (churchwarden of West Knoyle), Mr Davies (churchwarden of West Knoyle), Dr Longbourne (churchwarden of Mere), the Right Revd George Reindorp (Bishop of Salisbury), Revd John Smith, Ven. Basil Wingfield-Digby (Archdeacon of Sarum), Bishop Arthur (Rural Dean), Mr Cocke (churchwarden of Mere), His Grace the Duke of Somerset (churchwarden of Maiden Bradley).

Left: *Revd Ben Elliott 'surveying his parish from the church tower', 1992.*

Right: *The induction of Revd David Linaker as vicar of Mere, West Knoyle and Maiden Bradley, 1 July 1999. Left to right: Revd Michael Flight (Rural Dean), Revd David Linaker, Mrs Linaker, Ven. Barney Hopkinson (Archdeacon of Sarum.)*

date from that time. In the south-east corner is the mistakenly-named charnel house which is used as a store. Incorporated into it is a doorway and window rescued from the sixteenth-century Church House that stood nearby and which was demolished in 1890.

The known vicars of Mere are:

1300 Roger the Clerk
1331 Walter ?
1374 Richard Bisschop
1405 Nicholas Modeford
15?? John Swinnerton
1554 John Roberts
1556 Richard Chafyn
1586 Richard Potter
1630 Thomas Chafyn
1646 William Bayly
1691 Edward Garrard
1695 John Hardcastle
1734 Caleb Perfect
1744 Thomas Staples
1775 Charles Allix
1796 Lancelot Holton
1802 Thomas Grove
1809 William Hopkins
1812 Henry Wake
1845 Thomas Blundell
1861 Charles Townsend
1881 Edwin Wyld
1890 John Lloyd
1909 Francis Trotman
1927 Ian Cameron
1936 Norman Johnson
1965 Raymond Preston Thomas
1976 John Smith
1981 William (Ben) Elliott
1999 David Linaker

St Matthew's Church

Towards the end of the nineteenth century there was the need to offer people living in the Causeway and Limpers Hill a nearby place of worship. Money was raised and Miss Julia Chafyn Grove donated a site on the corner of the Shaftesbury Road and Wet Lane. A church was designed by C.E. Ponting and built by J. Hooper and C. Coward of Mere at a cost of £1,500. It was opened on St Matthew's Day 1882 and, under the ministry of the curate, the Revd William Chell, the church won a place in the affection of the people of the neighbourhood and flourished for many years. In 1941 it was temporarily closed and then reopened for occasional services in 1951. It was officially closed at the end of 1980 but following determined efforts by members of the congregation, reopened as an independent church under the supervision of the Bishop of Ramsbury in 1981. At the time of writing it has been decided that in September 2004 the church will finally close its doors.

St Matthew's Church, 1981.

Interior of St Matthew's Church.

The Roman Catholic Church

Until 1932 Roman Catholics in Mere were served by the priest at St Benedict's Church at Bonham, Stourton, who was based at Downside Abbey. Between 1932 and 1939 a room behind the Butt of Sherry in Castle Street was rented and used for services and then, for a time, a room in the Grove Buildings. In 1946 St Mary's Church in Pettridge Lane was opened on land given by a former resident of Mere in memory of her son killed at Dunkirk in 1940. It is a Nissen hut nicely converted and furnished, seating 80 people. The altar and Stations of the Cross were obtained from the private chapel at Fonthill Abbey. At the time of writing, priests from Wincanton serve there.

The United Reformed Church and the Methodist Church have been described in Chapter 6.

St Mary's Roman Catholic Church, 1997.

Chapter 10

Schools

It is recorded that in the early-seventeenth century, 'John Martin was a schoolmaster in a little market town called Meere in Wilts.' This comes from an account by his son, also John Martin, who, as rector of Compton Chamberlayne, was notorious in his resistance to the Commonwealth and was consequently deprived of his living. In 1680 George Gerard, schoolmaster, is mentioned in the parish register. Sir Matthew Andrews, who died in 1711, left an estate at Wolverton for the endowment of a free school in Mere. A school house was built and a schoolmaster appointed at a salary of £25 a year. This was paid only until 1716 when his son refused to continue with the charity.

By the will of Dr Thomas Tatum who died in 1765, £10 was paid annually to a schoolmaster in Mere for instructing ten poor boys between the ages of 8 and 13. Charles Glover was a schoolmaster for many years and he included these ten boys in his school of 20–40 boys. The £10 continued to be paid up until 1861, the money going to the National School after it was established in the town.

Before 1791, Nathaniel Goldsbrough, a member of a prominent local family, set up a school in the spacious loft of The Close, Church Street, advertising in *The Salisbury and Winchester Journal* in that year:

N. Goldsbrough takes this method of gratefully acknowledging the favours already conferred on him by the Parents and Guardians of youth entrusted to his care and humbly hopes for a continuance thereof; and begs leave to acquaint his friends and the public that his school will be open for the reception of young gentlemen after the present vacation, on Monday 16th January. Mere is a remarkably pleasant and healthy situation at the foot of the Wiltshire Plains.

Board and Education per ann. (washing included) £12.12.0. Admission £1.1.0.

In 1807 a Mr Robertson opened a school in Mere for:

young gentlemen who will be boarded and instructed in the Latin and English languages, Writing in the different hand, Arithmetic through all its branches with Mathematics and Book Keeping.

Terms 22 guineas per annum, no Entrance.

William Barnes, schoolmaster, c.1835.

At the start of 1823 William Barnes the Dorset poet, then aged 22, came to Mere to take over Mr Robertson's school. He took lodgings in Salisbury Street and advertised in *The Salisbury and Winchester Journal*:

Mere, Wilts. W. Barnes respectfully informs the inhabitants of Mere and its vicinity that he has opened a school in a commodious room over the Market Place in that town where he teaches Reading, Plain and Ornamental Penmanship, Geography, Arithmetic and English Grammar at 3 guineas per annum. W.B. avails himself of the present opportunity to express his gratitude to those who have already committed their children to his care and assures them and those who may be induced to favour him with their support hereafter that it shall be his endeavour by following the most approved modes of teaching and by unremitting exertion on his part to discharge his important trust to their satisfaction.

The schoolroom over the Market House had been used by Charles Glover and, presumably, by Mr Robertson before William Barnes took it over. In this upper storey was housed the town clock, so lessons were often given against a background of the loud ticking of the clock and a market hubbub below.

This drawing by William Barnes dates from c.1823. It shows the cross loft in the Market House, Mere, used by Barnes as a schoolroom.

The room was quite large, for it had served as a court house of the Duchy of Cornwall for over four centuries and even in Barnes' time, it made do in the evenings as the town's theatre. In May 1823, Barnes had 12 pupils and by August that year the total had reached 24. However, he had difficulty in ensuring the fees were paid. Some parents just took advantage of the inexperienced young schoolmaster, others demanded rebates because their boys were absent during haymaking whilst there were some, no doubt, who found it genuinely difficult to find the money from their farming or small business profits.

In 1827 William Barnes married and, with his wife Julia, moved into The Chantry which he rented from Miss Chafyn Grove for 20 guineas per year with the intention of taking boarders. The age of his pupils ranged from 6–14 and there was a maximum of 40 boys. By 1829 a postscript to his school advertisement read:

W.B. recommends his establishment to the notice of parents connected with foreign commerce as he is capable of teaching the Latin, French, Italian, Spanish, Portugese, German, Swedish and Danish languages.

To find a school of the 1820s in a small west of England town offering so much is surprising enough; even more so, when it is realised that all this was taught by one 28-year-old master.

William and Julia Barnes left Mere in June 1835 and moved to Dorchester to open a school there. Whilst in Mere, William had started writing his poems of rural life in the Dorset dialect. On leaving The Chantry he wrote the following poem, not in dialect:

To a Garden on Leaving It

Sweet garden! peaceful spot! No more in thee
Shall I e'er while away the sunny hour.
Farewell each blooming shrub and lofty tree;
Farewell the mossy path and nodding flower;

The Chantry, c.1830, from a watercolour painting by William Barnes.

73

The Grove Buildings are on the left, with the National School on the right. The National School was built in 1839, the Grove Buildings as a school annexe in 1891.

The unveiling of a plaque on the clock tower, Mere, in October 1986 to commemorate the centenary of the death of William Barnes. Left to right: District Councillor Jack Paul, the engraver Caroline Webb, Professor Peter Levi, Oxford Professor of Poetry.

The staff of the British School, late-nineteenth century. Left to right, back row: Mrs John Hooper (née Polly Farthing), Flo Maidment, Flo Carpenter, Miss Alexander, Mrs Skinner (née Miss A. Coward); front: Miss J. Hooper, the headmaster Mr Chard, Miss Wiltshire.

The British School, 1888–89.

I shall not hear again from yonder bower
The song of birds or humming of the bee,
Nor listen to the waterfall, nor see
The clouds float on behind the lofty tower.
No more, at breezy eve or dewy morn
My gliding scythe shall shear thy mossy green:
My busy hands shall never more adorn,
My eyes no more may see this peaceful scene.
But still, sweet spot, wherever I may be,
My love-led soul will wander back to thee.

Mere British, Mixed and Infant Schools, 1905.

Another private school was being run by the curate, Mr Cosens, living at the vicarage. In his advertisement of 1832 he said 'each boy would have his own bed', no reflection, one hopes, on any shortcomings in Mr Barnes' establishment, although it was quite common to crowd small boys into large beds in the cheaper schools. The competition between Barnes at The Chantry and Cosens across the road from him does not seem to have prevented them meeting socially: they played in string quartets together at The Chantry.

The *Salisbury and Winchester Journal* of 1842 carried this rather pompous advertisement:

Mere School, Conducted by Mr. J.A. Lander, Terms for Board and Instruction, Books, Perusal of Books in School Library and washing, £22 per annum. The above terms include every scholastic item. The experience Mr

Lander has acquired during the long period he was engaged as resident master in Collegiate, Metropolitan and other first-rate and extensive Establishments together with his adoption of the most approved and modern methods which he has successfully applied in the mathematical preparation of gentlemen for the universities, Naval and Military Colleges, etc., tends in no small degree to expedite the improvement of pupils committed to his charge. No limitation of diet. Surveying will be practically taught in the Field. A Christmas Examination Paper will be forwarded to any Parent on application.

A year later, Mr Lander moved to larger premises and his wife, with the help of a governess, undertook to take 'four to six young ladies'.

The National School, Mere: 'children who have made unbroken attendances during the year 1898'.

In 1852 Mrs Baverstock had a boarding- and day-school in Castle Street, in 1877 Mr Richard Rodman opened a boarding- and day-school in The Market Place and in the same year Miss Jane Cross began Prospect Villa School in Castle Hill Lane. In the 1890s Miss Somervale had a girls' school at The Grange, Water Street, and Mr Angrave, after being headmaster of the British School between 1889 and 1899, started a school of his own at Glebe House, Church Street. In 1908, Miss McLaughlin lived at The Chantry and, with her sister and an assistant, opened a school for 'Daughters of Friends and Others'.

Private efforts were also being made to teach poor children according to Nonconformist principles. David White had a small school in Salisbury Street and Thomas Denny began a school in the kitchen of Dewes House. When that was no longer large enough, Mr Denny moved the school into the coach-house there. Both the Congregational chapel and the St Michael's Parish Church had well-supported Sunday schools.

In 1833 the first state grant for education was introduced and an education enquiry was sent to overseers of the poor in every county to forward on to schools in their areas so that needs could be assessed. Ten returns were sent in from Mere. In August 1837 Dean Pearson of Salisbury preached in St Michael's Church stressing the need for a 'scriptural education' for the poorer classes. As a direct result of this, funds from the National Society for the Education of the Poor According to the Principles of the Church of England were made available and, with contributions from local people, a National

School was built on a site given by the Dean at the corner of Church Street and Barton Lane in 1839. It was opened by him in November 1840. Not to be outdone, the Congregational Church opened a day-school in a room adjoining their chapel in Boar Street in March 1840. It started with 26 children and its first master was Thomas Denny. In 1852, when a new Congregational chapel was built, a large schoolroom in the basement was provided for the children, which became known as the British School.

In 1864 the National School was enlarged by building an extra classroom to the north. In 1891 the Grove Buildings were erected, the cost of £2,400 being met by Miss Julia Chafyn Grove. This had two large rooms, which were used as an infant schoolroom and a technical room, as well as a small parish room (now the kitchen) with a separate entrance and a lobby. A playground on the opposite side of the road (now part of the garden of 1 Church Street) was later given to the school by Miss Chafyn Grove.

It was not until 1879 that education became compulsory in Mere and a School Attendance Officer was appointed. Before that, many children were 'half-timers' at school, being employed as child labour in the silk mills or on farms.

In 1902 the Balfour Education Act became law and all voluntary schools were made a charge on the rates. Nonconformists in Mere were indignant that public money should be used for sectarian purposes, meaning, presumably, that the rates should not support the religious instruction given by the Church of England in their schools. So strong was the objection that several people in Mere, including Dr Rutter,

The sale of goods by passive resisters to the Balfour Education Act of 1902.

Mere First School (the former Infants' School) in Dark Lane, c.1985.

Mr Muspratt's class, the National School, c.1919. Left to right, back row: ?, Harry Gould, Gordon Gatehouse, Harold Keats, ?, Leonard Gillard, Sydney Gray, Charles Gray, George Maidment, ?, Mr Muspratt; centre: ?, Leslie Mills, Louis Elsworth, Annie Sheppard, Marjorie Gray, Lily Maidment, Grace Lawrence, Nora Arnold, Fred Gould, ?; front: Dorothy Gatehouse, Fred Meatyard, Ivy Farthing, Alice Banning, Ethel Lawrence, Eva Hoskins, Olive Phripp, Betty Coward.

The school bus, c.1928.

became passive resisters to paying the education rate and had their goods distrained (some of the items sold were bought by the Lecture Hall, the Congregational Church and the Methodist Church). This opposition continued until 1914.

In 1907 the British School was forbidden by the Board of Education to use the infants' schoolroom because it was in a basement. The County Council refused to build a new room for them because there was enough space at the National School for all children of school age. The Board threatened to withdraw its grants to the school. In 1908 a meeting of parents and friends of the British School decided to build a new infants' school in Dark Lane and with donations and proceeds from bazaars, the cost of the building, £929, was met. The new school was opened in 1910; ownership was given to the Lecture Hall Trust who let it to the County Council at a peppercorn rent.

Mr Arthur White, joint chairman of the Mere Schools, 1922.

In 1921 a consultation document on the schools in Mere was sent by the County Director of Education to the managers of both Mere schools proposing that they amalgamate. At a combined managers' meeting it was agreed to accept the proposal so long as the religious differences were respected. The chairman of the new joint managers was Mr Arthur White of Charnage and at last, in 1922, the long-standing feud between church and chapel over education was resolved. The Church Street building became the Senior School, the Boar Street building became the Junior School and the combined Infants' School was accommodated in Dark Lane. In 1927 the school at West Knoyle closed and the children were transferred to Mere.

In 1929 the Senior School was renamed a Central School and provision was made to teach woodwork and domestic science in addition to ordinary subjects. In that year the number of school managers was increased to include representatives from Kilmington, Stourton and Zeals and, in 1930, from Maiden Bradley and Kingston Deverill too because senior children from these outlying parishes were included in the scheme. Between 1937 and 1940 arrangements were made for Wiltshire County Council to assume responsibility for the Mere

schools. Through the Education Act of 1944 the Senior School became a Secondary Modern School and children passing the 11-plus exam went on to Gillingham School. In 1946 a Central Kitchen was built in Pettridge Lane to supply meals to all the schools in the area.

In 1964 the foundation-stone for a new school building was laid at a site off Springfield Road leased from the Duchy of Cornwall. The school was officially opened in July 1966 and named the Duchy Manor Secondary School. It had a large assembly hall also used as a gymnasium, a science laboratory, craft and domestic-science rooms, a library and extensive playing-fields. A swimming pool was added, paid for out of a Town Swimming Pool Fund set up in 1935 to commemorate King George V's silver jubilee, with a grant from the County Council and by public subscriptions. In 1972 the school became a Middle School with an age range of 9–13 years, all pupils going on to Gillingham at 13.

In 1993 the Infants' School (by then called Mere First School) in Dark Lane closed and was relocated on the Duchy Manor School site. Further reorganisation in 2002 resulted in the First School (now Mere School) taking children up to the age of 11 and the Middle School winding down, with final closure in July 2004. All Mere children now attend Gillingham School after the age of 11.

The former Junior School is now a warehouse and showroom and the old Infants' School is a commercial store. The vacated National School in Church Street became a County Library in 1970 and Mere Museum was invited to share the building. In 2002 it became the Mere Information Point incorporating library, museum, the Tourist Information Office and other services. It is fitting that Dean Pearson's school should still be serving some educational purpose.

At the time of writing there is one private school in Mere, Stourbridge House School (a nursery and pre-preparatory school), which moved from Milton on Stour to Glebe House, Church Street in 1981. It caters for boys and girls between the ages of 2½ and 8 and there are about 60 pupils. It is a popular and successful school under the headship of Mrs Elisabeth Coward. There are also two playschools in Mere for the under-fives.

Mere Infants' School, 1933. Miss Minnie Bristow with the Baby Class. Left to right, back row: Miss Bristow, Jim Pike, ? Pugsley, Derek Topp, Brian Hembury, Ronald Bristow, George Pester; third row: Margaret Shergold, Greta Greenland, Jean Doddington, Audrey Brockway, Daphne Broadway, Nita Gould, Gwen Ings, Betty Arney, Betty Pike; second row: Eileen Norris, Doris Francis, Daisy ?, Dorothy Foot, Jean Parfitt, Mary Hansen; front: John Sams, ? Norris, Tony Morgan.

Mere Infants' School, c.1933. Miss Wilcox with the Middle Class. Left to right, back row: Miss Wilcox, Kenneth Deverill, John Gatehouse, ? Norris, Cyril Foot, Geoffrey Cowley, John Snook, Pat Austin; third row: Barbara Pester, Betty Maidment, Edna Burfitt, Jean Gray, Joan Long, June Gray, Glenys Austin, Grace Gray, Daisy Gatehouse; second row: Kathleen Forward, Joyce Sams, Betty Parfitt, Linda Wadman, Ruth Bond, Peggy Howell, Lucy Norris; front: Kenneth Chislett, Derek Fricker, Philip Norris, Tony Tun, Edgar Whitty.

Mere Infants' School, c.1933. Miss Rowden with the Top Class. Left to right, back row: Miss Rowden, Roy Cannings, Walter Penny, Jim Burt, Rowland Whitby, Alan Greenland, Jim Penny; centre: Ian Lawrence, Sylvia Wadman, Mary Pugsley, Betty Dean, Margery Gatehouse, Joan Arney, Hubert Sheppard; front: Olive Norris, Mary Snook, ?, ?, Mary Morgan.

Mere Junior School, c.1933. Left to right, back row: *David Ellis, Bernard Howell, John Taylor, Douglas Chislett, Cecil Ford, J. Ricketts;* third row: *Joan Gatehouse, J. Bristow, Joyce Broadway, Daisy Gatehouse, Pearl Riddy, Phyllis Root, Hazel Hembury, Betty Hansen, Hazel Penny, Sheila Pester, Benita Doddington;* second row: *Dorothy Whitty, Joyce Shergold, ?, Barbara Arney, Joan Hill, Joyce Francis;* front: *Philip Flower, Leslie Hooper, Stanley Ford, Kenneth Brockway, Roy Harrington, Reg Sams, Roy Hoskins, Dick Adams, George Langdon.*

Mere Secondary Modern School, first year pupils, c.1956.

The Duchy Manor School, 1974.

Mere First School, Class 1, 1983.

Mere First School, Class 2, 1983.

Mere First School, Class 3, 1983. The teacher is Mrs Holt.

Above: *Mere First School, Class 4, 1983. The teacher is Mrs Bundy.*

Right: *At Mere First School, 1987.*

Stourbridge House School pupils with their collage for an 'Aspects of Mere' competition in Mere Library/Museum, May 1992.

Chapter 11

Farming and Trade

From early times, any settlement would have had some sort of commercial centre but it was not until fairly recently that this would have been a collection of shops. In those early days people would have produced most of their own food and clothes, so commerce took the form of markets of surplus produce grown and manufactured within the area. From medieval times, markets were granted as a privilege to a town or village by the Crown or by the lord of the manor and these charters laid down rules about how they should operate. We have already seen that in 1408 King Henry IV granted his son, Henry, Duke of Cornwall, the right to have two fairs a year at Mere although the May fair lasted only until the eighteenth century. The August event seems to have been no more than a short visit from a travelling fair. In the nineteenth century, however, there were 'standings' near the clock tower where 'ginger bread, monkeys on sticks and cockles' were sold, as remembered by a contributor to *The Story of Mere*, published in 1958. It is interesting that at the end of the twentieth and start of the twenty-first centuries there has been a resurgence of farmers' markets in many parts of the country and that they are proving to be very successful.

In the fifteenth century there was a market cross in The Market Place and this was soon replaced by the Market House (previously mentioned in Chapters 3 and 6). The trade that took place at the Market House was mostly the selling of cattle, corn and other produce but we do not know when that trade ended. In 1799 a revival was attempted when Giles Jupe, bailiff of the manor, advertised 'a toll-free market for corn and cattle, to commence on Tuesday, January 7th, 1800'. The notice added as an inducement that 'good Ordinary (a farmers' lunch) would be on offer at the Ship at 1 o'clock'. This market does not seem to have prospered for in 1817 another attempt was made to have a 'Pitched Corn Market' each Monday. This lasted only a couple of years.

There is evidence that there was a weighbridge on the eastern side of the Market House before its demolition in 1863. Subsequently, there was a weighbridge

The weighbridge by the clock tower, c.1915.

Haymaking at Mere, late-nineteenth century.

operated by 'The Mere Weighbridge Company' on the corner of Castle Street and Barton Lane and when that land was sold in 1887 the weighbridge was transferred to just west of the clock tower. At that time, before the days of easy transport, a weighbridge was common in country towns, providing acceptable proof of the weight of cattle, corn, coal, etc.

In the early-fourteenth century the Earl of Cornwall used his land in the manor of Mere for keeping and breeding his horses. Oxen and sheep grazed his pastures and poultry was kept. The steward sold surplus cheese, butter, wheat and oats. In the fourteenth to seventeenth centuries when Mere had a flourishing wool trade, sheep farming was favoured. From the seventeenth to nineteenth centuries when flax weaving was a local industry, flax was grown; indeed a field at Lordsmead was known as Yarnfield, suggesting that flax was grown there.

The Duchy of Cornwall still owns much of the farm land in and around Mere. Manor Farm, Wood Farm, Mere Down Farm, Burton Farm, Chetcombe Farm, East and West Swainsford Farms and Hinks Mill Farm all have The Prince of Wales as their landlord. The largest farm in Mere in 2004 is at Charnage, owned and farmed by the White family over several generations. Prospect Farm at the western end of

Castle Street was part of the Zeals House estate and in the early-twentieth century was tenanted by Mr E.C. Sims who was a dairy farmer making cheese. Spare milk from the dairy farmers was taken to the milk factory in Water Street. A few farmers sold direct to London, putting their milk churns on the train at Gillingham Station.

At the time of writing, dairy herds are much bigger than they had traditionally been, primarily because of the amalgamation of smaller farms into bigger units and the mechanisation of milking, feeding and housing cows. Feed is mostly grass silage but many farms grow forage maize as well. The commonest breed of milking cows here are Friesan/Holstein and the milk quality and yield is very good. Beef cattle are grazed on downland too steep to plough; in the winter months they are kept under cover. Common breeds are Hereford and Aberdeen Angus. Sheep farming is still done on a relatively small scale although its popularity seems to be on the increase. In recent years several small farms have been sold because the farmers have found it uneconomic to continue; the land has gone to neighbouring farmers and the farmhouse, perhaps with two paddocks, has been transformed into a country house for newcomers.

Haymaking at Southbrook, Mere, late-nineteenth century.

Sheep dipping at Burton, 1907.

Wood Farm, 1998.

Mere Down Farm, 1998.

Burton Grange Farmhouse, 1998.

Chetcombe Farm, 1998.

Hinks Mill Farm, 1979.

Above: *Harvesting at Burton, c.1900.*

Right: *Town Mill, c.1970.*

Arable farming in this area mostly involves the growing of corn and a lot of winter wheat. Oil-seed rape and linseed are quite commonly seen and some oats and barley are grown. The production of crops is highly mechanised with large tractors and very large combine harvesters managed by a much smaller workforce than was needed in earlier years.

Parts of the farm land in Mere are now classified as Environmentally Sensitive Areas and Sites of Special Scientific Interest. At Mere Down Farm, Mr Colin Coward was runner-up in the 2003 Silver Lapwing Award which is given for outstanding conservation work in the UK to encourage wildlife and enrich the countryside.

Because of the abundance of water in the locality, Mere was able to support a fulling mill and several corn-mills in the fourteenth century. In 1280 there was already a corn-mill on the south side of the church (although this may have had horse power rather than a water-wheel) and where the Shreen and Ashfield Water join there was, later, the Town Mill which had sufficient water power to drive the mill day and night. The nineteenth-century miller George Dodd continued to grind corn at Town Mill until the first years of the twentieth century. At Lordsmead there was another corn-mill which became Henry Jupe's linen factory and at Hinks Mill was the nineteenth-century silk mill. The mill at Burton was mainly used for grinding chaff. At Rook Street was an ancient fulling mill, demolished in 1890.

Barley was an important crop in Wiltshire and until the early-nineteenth century there were maltings in Church Street, Manor Road, The Triangle and elsewhere in the town. One malt-house was established by the Lander family at the corner of Hazzards Hill and Water Street in the eighteenth century. Of the present buildings, owned by Yapp Bros. in 2004, that part facing Hazzards Hill was probably the malt-house, originally a long low building with small windows to give a wide area for spreading the steeped barley. In the 1830s, maltster Charles Lander became a brewer as well. The premises had the advantage of a supply of very clear water from a spring and the spring is there to this day. The brew house was probably in the building that is directly opposite the entrance archway on the eastern side of

The steam-driven lorry belonging to George Dodd of Town Mill, c.1915.

The mill-wheel at Lordsmead, c.1920.

The old mill-wheel at Burton, early-twentieth century.

the present courtyard. The brewery was never a large one and is likely to have limited its supplies to various small beer houses in the town and off-licence sales for home consumption. The Landers established their own 'tap bar' with a six-day licence trading under the name 'Ring of Bells' in part of the house facing Water Street. The brewery closed in 1885 after the death of Charles Lander and his sons Ernest and Charles reopened it as a bacon-curing factory, taking in George Tunstall as a partner. This business lasted only ten years and Ernest then turned his hand to the sale of milk and dairy products. In 1907 he sold the business to the milk products firm Prideaux at Motcombe. The milk factory prospered, especially during the two world wars when National Dried Milk was needed. In 1959 Cow & Gate took control but the premises were soon only used as a laboratory and experimental station. The milk factory closed down in 1970 and the site sold to a property development company. In 1973 Mr Robin Yapp bought it and renovated the old buildings, retaining the tall factory chimney. As a wine importer he commissioned a copy of the fountain that stands in the courtyard at Chateauneuf du Pape for his own courtyard and this is a distinctive feature of his renovated Old Brewery. Yapp Bros., who deal in imported Rhône and Loire wines, have an international reputation of excellence and have certainly helped to put Mere 'on the map'.

The bacon-curing factory at the Old Brewery, Water Street, c.1890.

Above: *Cheese making at the 'milk factory', c.1960. Wilf Lawrence is on the left and Tom Long is on the right.*

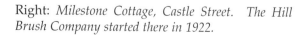

Above: *The courtyard at Yapp Bros, the Old Brewery, Water Street, c.1980.*

Right: *Milestone Cottage, Castle Street. The Hill Brush Company started there in 1922.*

Old brush-making machinery at the Hill Brush Company.

The important linen and silk industries of Mere have already been described in Chapter 6. Of more recent industries, the Hill Brush Company has an interesting history. In the early-twentieth century Arthur Coward had a wood-turning business in Castle Street producing toys, handles and brush backs. In 1922, after some early experiments, two of his sons, Fred and Bill, began making bass brooms for the wholesale trade, using a workshop in their father's yard. In 1925, two staff were employed and in 1927 this was increased to five. Shortly after that, two 14-year-old boys were taken on, one of whom, Walter Gatehouse, stayed with the company until his retirement in 1978, ending up as chief foreman. By 1927 a move to Lordsmead Mill was made where the water-wheel was used for driving the machinery. In 1930 the workforce had risen to 12. In 1935 the company moved to Woodlands Road and a factory was constructed on land rented from the Duchy of Cornwall. In 1941 the Duchy sold the land to them and the present (2004) buildings cover about 10 acres. In 1939 when the number of staff was 28, many of the men joined the services and as a result women were employed by the firm for the first time. In 1947 the first automatic broom-making machine was installed. By 1960 the number employed was 70, new buildings were being established and old machinery replaced.

The 1970s saw the company continuing to expand and nylon being used in place of many of the natural fibres used in brush making. In 1978 Hill Brush Company products were being sold to Buckingham Palace and Windsor Castle and in 1981 a Royal Warrant was granted to the company. At the time of writing male and female employees number 110. As well as making a wide variety of brushes, the firm also produces medical aids (bath seats, etc.), wine-bottle boxes, mops and cloths. There is a branch established in the USA and the company exports its products worldwide.

Next door to the Hill Brush Company in Woodlands Road, F.E. Beaumont Ltd, steel-chimney makers and steeplejacks arrived in 1968. They were important employers of local people and the factory's closure in the early-twenty-first century is much regretted. Beaumont's chimneys were exported to many countries and their low-loader lorries carrying very large sections of chimneys were a familiar sight in the town. Their factory has now been converted into several business units and Beaumont Specialist Fabrication Ltd (not part of F.E. Beaumont) is in one section, employing 11 staff, making chimneys on a small scale.

There is a small industrial estate at the former Dead Maid Quarry on the western side of Mere. A great variety of small businesses are there with a sizeable candle factory and a light-fitting factory.

A market-gardening business was founded in 1899 by George Burden. He came to Mere as gardener to Mr Rutter at Dewes House and, after the death of his employer, he set up his own business of growing and selling plants and flowers. With the help of his four sons the nursery flourished, greenhouses were built in North Street and in the early 1900s most villages within seven miles were regularly visited by the boys pushing hand carts loaded with plants, flowers and seeds. In about 1913, the two eldest sons left to start their own businesses, Walter to Ashwell, Mere, and Edward to Salisbury. The two younger sons, Gideon and Henry, worked

New brush-making machinery at the Hill Brush Company, 1988.

The 'front door' of the Hill Brush Company, Woodlands Road, 1998.

F.E. Beaumont's steel-chimney factory in Woodlands Road, 1980.

Mr and Mrs George Burden and family, c.1893. Left to right, back row: *Edward, Adeline, Gideon, Walter;* front: *Henry, Jane, Bessie, George, Sally.*

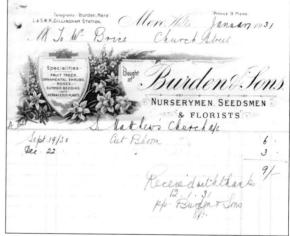

Billhead for Burden & Sons, 1931.

Henry Burden in his father's greenhouse in North Street, c.1900.

Walter Burden's greenhouses at Burton Field, c.1940.

with their father in landscaping and nursery work. In the late 1920s, Walter extended his greenhouses into Burton Field to grow great quantities of tomatoes and, by using the plentiful water supply, watercress. He was succeeded there by his sons Bill, Jack and Roy. These Burton Field greenhouses are, alas, derelict in 2004. Henry and Gideon built greenhouses on the western side of Mere at Townsend where, suiting the chalky soil, tomatoes, cucumbers, chrysanthemums, carnations and lilies were grown. Today, Henry's grandsons run North Street Nurseries and J.B. Plants and a shop on the original North Street site continues to sell flowers, pot plants, vegetables and gardening sundries. J.B. Plants now has several very large modern greenhouses growing thousands of pot plants at Townsend. Some of Burdens' watercress beds are now used by Mere Fish Farm to breed trout.

The handsome eighteenth-century stone-built Old Ship Hotel is described in Chapter 5. Standing approximately opposite to it on the western side of The Square is the George Inn, which is thought to date from 1580. It is also stone built but it is faced with plaster and timbering which dates only from a 1920s renovation. It was, from about 1822 until 2002, known as the Talbot Hotel. The talbot dog was the crest of the Chafyn Grove family who leased the property between 1711 and 1866. The family bought the freehold in 1866. The Talbot was one of the centres of Mere life; it was a regular venue for auction sales and similar events and after 1863 the Duchy's Manorial Court, formerly meeting in the Market House, met at the Talbot. In the early-twentieth

A modern greenhouse for J.B. Plants at Townsend, 1998.

century it was exceptional in its provision of garage facilities for its customers and it is from this that the name of the present-day Talbot Garage owned by F.J. Chalke Ltd, is derived. On the north side of the Talbot Hotel were outbuildings, a brew house and cottages that were demolished in 1968 for road widening. One small part of these buildings was occupied in 1848 by Albert Bioletti, a hairdresser.

In 1848 Mrs Amelia Larkham, a widow, set up as a spirit dealer in Castle Street with her son Edward. She continued in this business until her death in 1878 after which Edward traded under his own name. On his death in 1894 the property was bought for £440 by Mrs Constance Hartgill of the Bell & Crown Inn, Zeals, who opened it as a public house, the Butt of Sherry. In 1918 it was sold to the Lamb Brewery of Frome and in 2004 owned by Gibbs Mew of Salisbury. The premises included, on the western side of the public house, a tailor's shop since 1784 in

Burden & Sons' greenhouses at Townsend, c.1960.

The dining-room at the Old Ship Hotel, early-twentieth century.

The Talbot Hotel, now the George Inn, and the Old Ship Hotel, c.1960.

The Talbot Garage (F.J. Chalke), Salisbury Street, 1997.

the ownership of the Baverstock family. They sold it to the brewers during the Second World War.

The original Walnut Tree Inn on the Shaftesbury Road was built in about 1840 and stood on the roadside. It was pulled down in 1938 and replaced by a new one on land above and behind it. In its early days it was owned by Flower's Brewery at Fontmell Magna, then by Matthew's Brewery of Gillingham which has since been absorbed into Hall and Woodhouse of Blandford. At the time of writing the building is soon to be demolished for housing and a replacement built once more by the roadside.

The Angel Inn stood on the south side of The Square opposite the clock tower. Its original frontage ran from Angel Lane eastwards to include the present supermarket site but all this was demolished in the nineteenth century and rebuilt. In 1881 the whole site was sold and only a small portion of it along Angel Lane with a narrow part facing The Square was kept and opened as a public house in 1883. The easternmost part of the site was bought for the erection of the Victoria Hall in 1899. Between the new Angel Inn and the hall a Temperance Hotel was established by J.F. Rutter, the solicitor; by the 1930s this had become the Central Hotel, the proprietor being Andrew F. Chalke. In 2004 this building is occupied by R. & M. Cockram, ironmongers. The Angel Inn continued in business until 1969. It was then kept as an off-licence by Hall & Woodhouse until 1993 when it became a shoe shop. In 2004 it is the Angel Corner Tea Room.

At the rear of the Angel Inn there was a fives court and a buttressed wall still stands there. The date of its construction is not known but the game was certainly played in Mere in the eighteenth and early-nineteenth centuries. It was played by striking

A 1936 photo of the original Walnut Tree Inn, demolished in 1938.

a 2-inch-diameter leather-covered ball with the hand. Courts could be found in the yards of many inns in this part of the country. For example, behind the Fleur de Lis Hotel at Stoke sub Hamdon a particularly fine fives wall survives.

The White Hart Inn in The Market Place was demolished in 1860 and the Swan Inn in Salisbury Street was demolished in 1863. In 1756 Thomas Carter is known to have been landlord of the Green Dragon and it was probably more of a beer house than an inn. It stood at the bottom of Steep Street on the southern side, near the old ford. At the junction of Warminster Hollow and the Salisbury Road once stood the Castle Inn. It seems to have closed in the early-nineteenth century and Castle House (demolished for the building of Mere bypass) was built either in place of it or next to it. The oddly named Gaping Goose at Whitehill was probably built in the mid-nineteenth century, for in 1848 the site was still farm land and in the 1860s the licence is known to

The Butt of Sherry, Castle Street, c.1900.

Above: *The Walnut Tree, 1990.*

The Angel Inn, c.1965.

The Victoria Hall when it was used as a cinema, c.1950.

A meet of the South & West Wilts Hunt outside the Central Hotel, c.1930.

have ended. It is supposed that the inn became the house now known as Belbins House.

In the last half of the nineteenth century and first half of the twentieth, John Walton & Co. dominated the retail trade in Mere. Its history has been described in Chapter 6. To the north of the clock tower on the corner of Manor Road (a Costcutter supermarket in 2004) is where John Walton's main store stood and it is here that Walton's predecessor, Charles Card, had his grocery and draper's business in a much smaller building. Charles Card was the local agent for the Wiltshire & Dorset Bank and when a Mere branch of the bank was opened, he was appointed manager. At first the bank operated within Card's shop but in 1858 he built the present bank premises and leased the site to the Wiltshire & Dorset until the bank bought the freehold from him in 1879. In 1914 Lloyds Bank took over the business which continues there to this day.

On the eastern side of Walton's shop is where Cullingford's Carpets were trading until 2002. It was once the home of John Walton and for many years Mere Post Office was run from this site. Next to this is the handsome house with bay windows, a charity shop at the time of writing, which was once the board-

The bottom of Steep Street with the former Green Dragon on the left, late-nineteenth century.

room and offices of Walton's. East of this is a site that formerly belonged to the Marquis of Bath and on which the White Hart Inn stood. After the inn was demolished Charles Card built two houses which were then bought by John Walton, one being given a shop front and used as a men's outfitters, the other let as a dwelling, at one time occupied by the local vet, Mr Charles Dewey.

Next to this, in the late-nineteenth century, was a picturesque two-storey thatched building which was the shop of 'Foot, late Maidment, Corn Factor, Baker, etc.' In about 1900 it was replaced by the tall red-brick building which, in the early-twentieth century, was a barber's and tobacconist's shop. It was then taken over as Walton's newsagent's department before becoming their pharmacy. In 2004 it is Jackson's Pharmacy.

On the south side of The Square is an attractive house with dormer windows, now 4 The Square, and next to it the shop of Robert Finan, the antiques auctioneer and valuer. In the eighteenth century the Hooper family was in business there as linen and woollen drapers, mercers and grocers. In 1812 it was taken over by John Curtis and then by his nephew's widow who married George Athoe, a

A design by William Barnes for a trade card for his friend Charles Card, grocer of Mere, c.1840.

The grocery department of John Walton & Co., c.1930.

Lloyds Bank next to the Old Ship Hotel, c.1912.

The Square, showing the ivy-covered house where John Walton had his home. It was also the home of Mere Post Office.

grocer from Pembrokeshire. Athoe's business continued until 1894 when John Walton acquired the shop and installed an ironmongery department there. It remained as an ironmonger's, eventually in the ownership of R. & M. Cockram who, in 1990, transferred the business to the former Temperance Hotel building nearby. Finan & Co. bought the former ironmongery and expertly renovated the shop front; this business continues to trade there in 2004.

THE WILTS AND DORSET STORES, MERE, WILTS.

BRANCHES AT | LONDON. | MAIDEN-BRADLEY, WILTS. | BOURTON, DORSET. | ZEALS, WILTS. | SEDGHILL, WILTS.

Established A.D. 1814

189

M

Dr. to JOHN WALTON & CO.,

WILTSHIRE BACON CURERS, CHEDDAR AND STILTON CHEESE FACTORS.

TERMS: 2 months, Nett Cash; or 1½ per cent. for cash within 10 days

Tea Merchants and Blenders.

No Carriage Paid on Orders under 1 cwt.

DORSET AND IRISH BUTTERS.

A billhead for John Walton & Co., 1890.

To the east of Finan & Co. is Squires' fruit and greengrocery shop housed in an Edwardian-style gabled building. In an early photograph of The Square there is on this site a low thatched house with a bay window, presumably a shop window. Mrs Charlton was trading there as a grocer in 1891, then by 1905 it was Applin's, grocers, drapers and milliners. In about 1912 the present shop must have been built and in the 1920s Applin's were advertising themselves as selling 'grocery, fruit, confectionery and ice cream' and having refreshment and tea rooms. This was also acquired by Walton's as an extension to their ironmongery department.

On the east side of Squires' shop is The Old Bakery. In 1910 it was occupied by Arthur Coward, builder and decorator, who later moved to Castle

Street to set up his wood-turning business there. In 1925 Mr Bert Stainer, who had a bakery in Hazzards Hill, transferred his shop to this site and it remained as Stainer's bakery until 1978. The site of the present John Walton's and Post Office was, until the 1960s, a small greengrocer's shop run by Mr Reg Doddington. After his death it was bought by Mr Peter Brewer who opened the Mini Mart, Mere's first supermarket, on the site. This continued until 1985 when Andrew Young, general manager of Walton's, took over the Post Office and built the present shop and a house for his family next door to it.

In the 1861 census Edwin Bracher, chemist, appears as living at The Triangle, the old Tudor house on the eastern side of The Square that was demolished in 1962. His billhead of 1885 describes him as 'Dispensing Chemist, Printer, Bookseller, Stationer and Bookbinder, Dealer in Oils, Colours, Paints, Varnishes, Painter's brushes, etc.' In the 1870s Bracher took on as his assistant Herbert H. Edmunds

Walton's Stores, the Talbot and Old Ship Hotels, Mere, c.1950.

Jackson's Pharmacy, 1998. This building replaced the shop of 'Foot late Maidment' in about 1900.

The shop of 'Foot late Maidment' in The Market Place, 1885.

Salisbury Street c.1925.

Shops on the south side of The Square in the late-nineteenth century. On the left is Charlton's, grocers, and next to it Athoe's, grocers and drapers.

The Mini Mart, c.1980.

A paper bag from Stainer's bakery.

The Square after 1894 when John Walton had installed his ironmongery department in Athoe's shop (Finan's in 2004).

and when the former retired in 1885, Edmunds succeeded to the business and lived on site. In 1911 the chemist's shop and printing works moved to Castleton House, Castle Street. In 1927 when Edmunds retired, the pharmacy was sold and in 1948 it was bought by Walton's, who, at some time over the following decade, moved it to The Square (where Jackson's Pharmacy is located in 2004). Herbert Edmunds' son Ewing continued to run the printing business as The Crown Printing Works in outbuildings at the rear of Castleton House with a frontage in Castle Hill Lane. He retired in 1949, selling the business to Jim Denslow, an employee, who continued as Mere's printer until his retirement in the 1970s.

In 1917 Mrs Denslow, mother of Jim, a war widow, came to Mere from Chard. She set up business in a building at the back of the Old Ship Hotel doing repair work on lace made by Bowden & Co. of Chard. The lace came from Chard by train to Gillingham and on completion was returned to Chard. Up to 30 girls were employed at one time.

After Edmunds left The Triangle it was used by John Walton & Co. to display and sell antiques

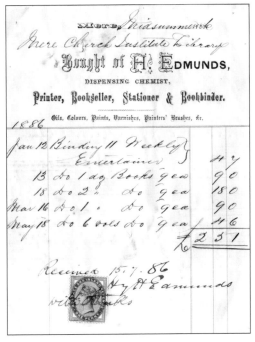

Billhead for H. Edmunds, chemist and printer, 1886.

before it became their newsagent's and tobacconist's when the pharmacy moved to The Square. At the rear of The Triangle was the Tudor Tea Rooms run by Miss Dodd which later moved to the Old House in Church Street.

In Salisbury Street the Mere & District Co-operative Society started trading in 1890 in the former Swan Coffee House, now Gilyard Scarth estate agents' office. In 1909 they transferred to the opposite side of the road in what is now a restaurant with groceries on the ground floor and furniture on the first floor. The Co-op's butcher's department was in a small shop nearer to The Square and its bakery was located in the shop that in 2004 is Jill Christie's hair salon. The Co-op had a slaughterhouse, warehouse and transport department in Water Street. In one of the houses between the Lecture Hall and The Square lived Mr Vic Humphries who had in his front room a barber's shop for many years up to the 1970s.

T.J. Norris, landlord of the Talbot Hotel and George Norris, an electrician in Church Street, ran a cinema in Mere in the early 1920s in the Victoria Hall. Charlie Jeans, then aged about 16, helped them and later, with Arthur Hames, took over the cinemas in

Edmunds' pharmacy in Castle Street, 1923.

John Walton's newsagents' shop at The Triangle, c.1945.

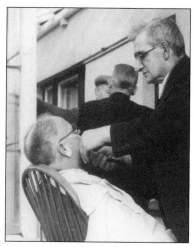

Vic Humphries, barber, Salisbury Street, 1953.

Above: *The Co-op store in Salisbury Street, c.1910.*

Mr and Mrs Welch and daughter outside their motor and cycle accessories shop in Salisbury Street, c.1928.

Jeans' electrical goods supplier (formerly Welch's), Salisbury Street, 1998.

Mere, Tisbury, Stalbridge and Sturminster Newton. In about 1960 the cinemas closed. Meanwhile, Charlie developed a business in radio, television and electrical goods, at first in a garage in Salisbury Street and then in the present premises near the town car park (which had been Welch's motor and cycle engineer's shop). In 2004 Charlie's son, George, owns and runs the business, which prospers, and he has a showroom in the old chapel (which was later the Junior School) in Dark Lane.

For the first years of the twentieth century there were four shoeing smiths in Mere: Ernest Whitmarsh in Castle Street, Harry Ford in Castle Hill Lane, Fred Sheppard in Salisbury Street and Robert Alford at Edgebridge. Only the sons of Whitmarsh and Ford continued as blacksmiths up to the 1960s and Whitmarsh's diversified into motor engineering with two petrol pumps at the roadside. Whitmarsh's forge and workshops were demolished for road widening in 1968. Another smith was Mr Sidney Howell at Southbrook who made and repaired tools and did wrought-iron work. One of his iron bridges still exists at Waterside Villa. James Down at Edgebridge was an edge-tool maker in the middle of the nineteenth century. His tools were mainly for agricultural work and a small number of such items bearing his name are in the collection of Mere Museum. His workshop was probably on the south-west side of the bridge where he could make use of a water-wheel powered by the River Shreen.

In the early-twentieth century there were three saddle- and harness-making businesses in Castle Street. Mr Dean lived at Milestone and his saddlery shop window can still be seen at the time of writing, although it now fronts a private house. William and George Stone were on the opposite side of the road, now The Old Saddlers, and a model of a white horse that stood in the window is a valued item owned by Mere Museum. Mr Thomas Standerwick had his saddlery workshop opposite his house, Yew Glen, in Castle Street.

Frederick Holmes was a photographer with his studio in Castle Street during the first quarter of the twentieth century. He produced a great quantity of picture postcards of Mere which provides us with a wonderful record of life here at that time. He was famous for his photograph of lightning at Mere taken to win a competition in May 1906.

William Lander was born in 1763. He set up in Castle Street as a brazier, producing a wide variety of household goods – bells, candlesticks, tea caddies, etc. – and farm and dairy utensils. He devised all sorts of machinery, such as pumps for wells and fire-engines. He also invented a 'waywiser', a wheeled machine for surveyors to measure distances; one of these is in the collection of Salisbury Museum. He submitted a design for a new bridge at Clifton, Bristol, but Brunel's design was chosen. He retired from business in 1833 and published a number of religious books. Two more generations of Landers continued as water and gas engineers and ironmongers. William Lander died in 1843 and is buried near the yew tree in Mere churchyard. His house in Castle Street, now Lander House, has a commemorative plaque affixed to it which records 'William Lander, 1763–1843, inventor, lived here'.

Other prominent craftsmen and tradesmen in the town included Mr Dismore of Castle Street who was a tinsmith making kettles and kitchenware and Mr Perman Maidment, wheelwright at Burton, whose father and son were also wheelwrights. Their workshop, unused at the time of writing but still displaying wheelwright's tools, is opposite the old sheepwash.

In 1852 there were, in Mere, the following traders and professional men listed in *Slater's Directory*:

1 *Brewer and beer retailer*
3 *Butchers*
7 *Bakers*
4 *Blacksmiths*
2 *Carpenters*
1 *Cabinet maker*
1 *Cheese factor*
1 *Chemist*
1 *Confectioner*
1 *Cooper*
1 *Currier and glover*
1 *Draper and grocer*
3 *Grocers*
1 *Gunsmith*
1 *Hairdresser*
1 *Hatter*
1 *Horse hirer*
1 *Ironmonger*
5 *Innkeepers*
2 *Joiners and wheelwrights*
1 *Miller*
2 *Masons*
1 *Maltster*
1 *Marine store dealer*
2 *Milliners and dressmakers*
1 *Painter and glazier*
1 *Plumber and hairdresser*
2 *Saddlers*
4 *Shopkeepers*
1 *Solicitor*
1 *Spirit dealer*
1 *Straw bonnet maker*
2 *Surgeons*
1 *Shoemaker*
5 *Tailors*
2 *Watchmakers*

This is a formidable list for a small country town. Today, Mere has comparatively few shops but there are many small businesses which, although not named in this chapter, are nevertheless valued contributors to the well-being of the community.

Welch's Garage, Hazzards Hill, early-twentieth century.

Whitmarsh's forge and garage, Castle Street, c.1930.

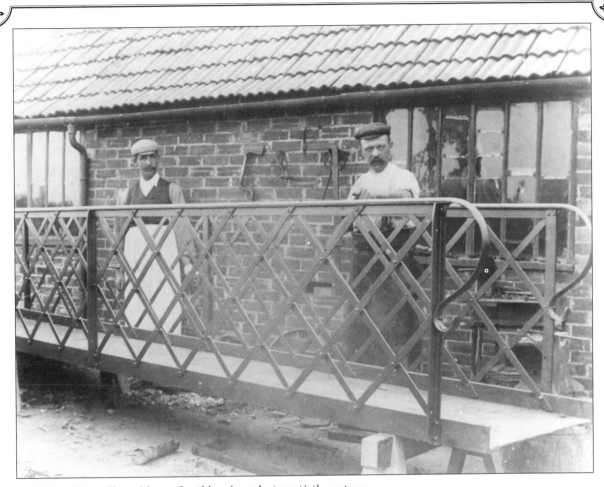

At Sidney Howell's smithy at Southbrook, early-twentieth century.

The old smithy at Southbrook, c.1969.

Stone's saddler's and harness-maker's shop, Castle Street. This display was to celebrate King Edward VII's coronation, 1902.

Stone's saddler's shop showing the model of a white horse in the window, 1956.

Thomas Standerwick's house, Yew Glen, and his workshop opposite it in Castle Street, late-nineteenth century.

Label for F. Holmes, photographer of Mere.

The famous photograph of lightning at Mere taken by Frederick Holmes on 13 May 1906.

An 1831 portrait of William Lander, brazier and inventor, aged 68.

Lander House, Castle Street, 1986. This was once the home of William Lander.

Mr Perman Maidment's wheelwright's workshop at Burton, c.1950.

Mr Arthur Maidment in the old wheelwright's workshop at Burton, 1998.

Matthew Norris' baker's shop, Salisbury Street, c.1907.

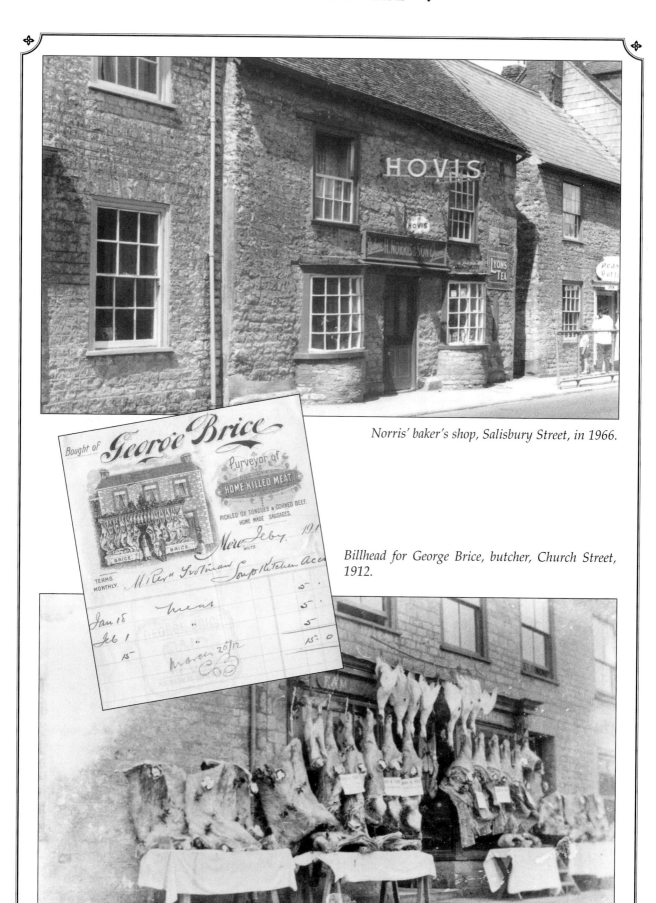

Norris' baker's shop, Salisbury Street, in 1966.

Billhead for George Brice, butcher, Church Street, 1912.

Christmas display at Brice's butcher's shop, Church Street, early-twentieth century.

W. Humphries, barber and tobacconist, Castle Street, c.1910.

Mr Thompson, taxidermist, Salisbury Street, early-twentieth century.

Edmunds' sweet shop, Castle Street, c.1938.

The shop of Redvers Pike, painter and decorator, Castle Street.

Mr and Mrs Frank Stone at the door of their grocery shop in Castle Street in the 1950s.

Monica Pester at her greengrocer's shop in The Square, c.1935.

Donkey cart belonging to G. Bristow, general dealer, c.1912. Fred Bristow is in the cart, Jerome Gatehouse is standing.

An itinerant knife-grinder, Mr Gatehouse, 1912.

Road making in Mere, 1895–1900.

E. R. JEANS,
Baker, Pastrycook & Confectioner,
Salisbury St. Mere.

MADEIRA, ALMOND, CHERRY and
GENOA CAKES, always to select from.
ALSO A LARGE VARIETY OF FANCY
CAKES MADE FRESH DAILY, AND OF
THE BEST QUALITY OBTAINABLE.

TRY THE IDEAL 'EURISSA'
WHITE BREAD, MADE ONLY
BY E. R. JEANS.

Turog, Home-made and Currant Bread made daily.

Orders by Post receive Prompt Attention.

GEORGE BRICE,
Family Butcher,

MERE, WILTS.

FAMILIES SUPPLIED WITH HOME-CURED

MEAT OF THE FINEST QUALITY.

Families waited on for Orders.

SALISBURY STREET, MERE, WILTS.

DISMORE & SON,
IRONMONGER, PLUMBER & GASFITTER,
BELL-HANGER,
Copper, Zinc, Tin and Iron Plate Workers,
CASTLE ST., MERE.

DAIRY UTENSILS MADE TO ORDER.

Cash Supply Stores,
R. & E. DAY,
Drapers, Milliners, Ladies' and
Children's Outfitters
SALISBURY STREET, MERE.

Orders by post receive special attention.
Clubs and Charities served.

S. BRISTOW,
TAILOR, ETC,

Has Patterns for all Classes, Suitable for all kinds of
wear, and all kinds of weather.

Customers' Wishes Carefully Studied.

'CASTLE' PLATE WORKS. MERE, WILTS

A Choice selection of Jewellery and Plate
at
can be seen at

COMPETITIVE PRICES,

S. HOOPER & SON,
WATCHMAKERS, JEWELLERS AND SILVERSMITHS,

The Leading House for repairs.

*A selection of advertisements for Mere tradesmen
from the year 1911.*

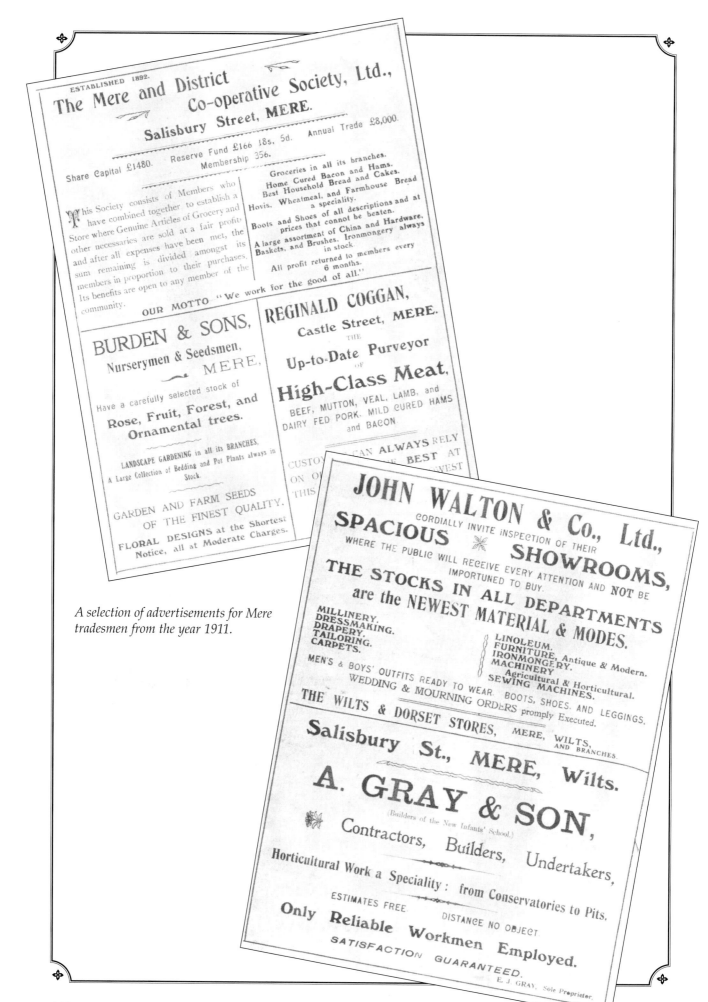

ESTABLISHED 1892.

The Mere and District Co-operative Society, Ltd.,

Salisbury Street, MERE.

Share Capital £1480.   Reserve Fund £166 18s, 5d.   Annual Trade £8,000.
Membership 356.

This Society consists of Members who have combined together to establish a Store where Genuine Articles of Grocery and other necessaries are sold at a fair profit, and after all expenses have been met, the sum remaining is divided amongst its members in proportion to their purchases. Its benefits are open to any member of the community.

Groceries in all its branches.
Home Cured Bacon and Hams.
Best Household Bread and Cakes.
Hovis, Wheatmeal, and Farmhouse Bread a speciality.
Boots and Shoes of all descriptions and at prices that cannot be beaten.
A large assortment of China and Hardware, Baskets, and Brushes. Ironmongery always in stock.

All profit returned to members every 6 months.

OUR MOTTO "We work for the good of all."

BURDEN & SONS,

Nurserymen & Seedsmen,
MERE,

Have a carefully selected stock of

Rose, Fruit, Forest, and Ornamental trees.

LANDSCAPE GARDENING in all its BRANCHES.
A Large Collection of Bedding and Pot Plants always in Stock.

GARDEN AND FARM SEEDS
OF THE FINEST QUALITY.

FLORAL DESIGNS at the Shortest Notice, all at Moderate Charges.

REGINALD COGGAN,

Castle Street, MERE.

THE

Up-to-Date Purveyor

OF

High-Class Meat,

BEEF, MUTTON, VEAL, LAMB, and DAIRY FED PORK. MILD CURED HAMS and BACON

CUSTOM...CAN ALWAYS RELY...BEST AT...WEST
ON O...
THIS...

A selection of advertisements for Mere tradesmen from the year 1911.

JOHN WALTON & Co., Ltd.,

CORDIALLY INVITE INSPECTION OF THEIR

SPACIOUS SHOWROOMS,

WHERE THE PUBLIC WILL RECEIVE EVERY ATTENTION AND NOT BE IMPORTUNED TO BUY.

THE STOCKS IN ALL DEPARTMENTS
are the NEWEST MATERIAL & MODES.

MILLINERY.
DRESSMAKING.
DRAPERY.
TAILORING.
CARPETS.

LINOLEUM.
FURNITURE, Antique & Modern.
IRONMONGERY.
MACHINERY.
Agricultural & Horticultural.
SEWING MACHINES.

MEN'S & BOYS' OUTFITS READY TO WEAR.   BOOTS, SHOES, AND LEGGINGS.
WEDDING & MOURNING ORDERS promply Executed.

THE WILTS & DORSET STORES,   MERE, WILTS,
AND BRANCHES.

Salisbury St., MERE, Wilts.

A. GRAY & SON,

(Builders of the New Infants' School.)

Contractors, Builders, Undertakers,

Horticultural Work a Speciality : from Conservatories to Pits.

ESTIMATES FREE.   DISTANCE NO OBJECT.

Only Reliable Workmen Employed.

SATISFACTION GUARANTEED.

E. J. GRAY, Sole Proprietor.

The Square, c.1921.

The Square and Salisbury Street, 1933.

Chapter 12

Clubs and Societies

Mere has a long tradition of supporting a large number of voluntary organisations in relation to its size, probably the result of being a somewhat isolated community relying on its own entertainment. The oldest record of such a group is that of a Mere branch of the British and Foreign Bible Society, formed in 1819 and meeting, surprisingly, at the Assembly Rooms of the Old Ship Hotel. That was also the place where, in 1877, the comic drama *The Spectre Bridegroom* and the farces *More than Welcome* and *Cherry Bounce* were presented. Presumably these were plays by the local drama group but Mere Drama Society was not properly established until November 1946 when Beryl Gray, a local teacher, got performers together to put on three one-act plays in the spring of 1947. From that beginning, the society has continued with regular spring and autumn productions at the Lecture Hall. In 1951 Mere Drama Society initiated and hosted a non-competitive One-Act Play Festival attended by seven other drama groups and this was the first of many entries by Mere players in local festivals. In 1996 the society celebrated its golden jubilee with an exhibition in Mere Museum, a production of the play *The Happiest Days of Your Life* and a Christmas concert at the Parish Church.

In October 1857 the Mere Ladies' Dorcas Society was formed for the benefit of 'poor women lying in', providing them with such essentials as a bag of baby linen. It was a sewing group of six or seven ladies who met at the vicarage once a month. It was later continued as a Mothers' Meeting held at the Lecture Hall. The group continued to meet until the 1920s.

In 1876 Mary Sumner, wife of the rector of Old Alresford, Hampshire, founded a fellowship of Christian mothers which at first was called the Women's Union. In 1911 a Women's Union branch was started in Mere at the suggestion of the Revd Francis Trotman, the vicar, and his wife. In 1914 the parish magazine reminded members that Lady Day, 25 March, was to be observed wherever the Union

Mere Drama Society performed Fools Rush In, *1959.* Left to right, standing: *Suzette Parsons, Alan Greenland, Douglas Lawley, Audrey Peers, Olive Langton, Dorothy George;* sitting: *Julie Coward, Jimmy Doddington.*

Mere Drama Society in When we are Married, 1976. Left to right, standing: *Trevor Truran, Sam Pryke, Sue Evans, Pip Potter, Dorothy George, Adrienne Howell, Edina Henderson, David Jukes, Peter Brewer, Mark Hebditch, Douglas Lawley;* sitting: *Betty Smith, Jeanette Francis, Olive Langton.*

The Mothers' Meeting (a sewing group) pictured in the garden of Dewes House in the late-nineteenth century.

Young members of the Mere Mothers' Union with toys they had made for a children's home, c.1958. Mrs Blandford Matthews, the Presiding Member for the Deanery, is holding the bouquet and Mrs Johnson, the vicar's wife, is standing on the far left.

Mothers with children who had been christened in Mere Church during the previous five years, entertained by Mere Mothers' Union, 1986.

existed as 'a day for corporate intercession and communion'. By 1918 the organisation was called the Mothers' Union and in 1923, 7,000 members in the Salisbury Diocese met at a great service in the cathedral. So many members attended that the service had to be repeated on the same day so that everyone who wanted to participate was able to do so. Local groups were encouraged to hold annual festivals in their rural deaneries – a tradition that continues to this day. Meetings of Mere MU are held once a month at the Grove Buildings with a guest speaker. The leaders of the Mere branch have been: Mrs E. Johnson, 1936–65; Mrs D. Thomas, 1965–76; Mrs J. Smith, 1976–79; Mrs J. Coward, 1979–86; Mrs M. Longbourne, 1986–92; Mrs M. Chalke, 1992–94. Mrs Thelma Ings, the leader at the time of writing, has occupied the position since 1994.

A Mere Nursing Association was founded in 1902 and it supported the work of a Mere district nurse, notably Nurse Wells who, over 39 years, gave devoted service as nurse and midwife. In 1937 an infant welfare clinic for mothers and babies was started by Mrs Glaisyer who, with helpers, ran it for 20 years. It continued regularly at the Lecture Hall and later, under the supervision of the health visitor, until about 1990.

The Mere Temperance Society, founded in 1840, had a large membership with monthly meetings for tea and lectures and annual excursions to the seaside and elsewhere. The Church of England Temperance Society was formed in 1882 and the Band of Hope for boys and girls ran concurrently with both societies.

A Mere Choral Society was formed

Nurse Wells, District Nurse in Mere, 1897–1936.

in 1882 and continued into the twentieth century under the direction of Mr Cope. In the 1950s and 1960s it was conducted by Ada Hooper, followed by Freddie Filor and Harold Bristow. The society continued to give concerts until about 1980. At the time of writing the town is the home of two groups of singers, Shreen Harmony, directed by Helen Porter, and Mere Chorale, conducted by John Isom.

Brass bands have played an important part in many local events. A Church of England Temperance Band was formed in 1883 and led the way for processions through the town for the jubilee celebrations of 1887 and 1897. In 1927 it became Mere Town Silver Band with Frank Sheppard as bandmaster and from about 1940–76 it was led by Archie Ford. In 1950 Adrienne Howell was the first woman to join. The band discontinued after 1986.

A Mere Junior Band was begun in 1963 and was succeeded by Mere Manor Youth Band founded by Adrienne and Bernard Howell in 1967. A committee of parents and members worked hard to fund the purchase of instruments and Adrienne taught the young members and conducted the band. Bernard, a cornet player, kept the instruments and equipment in good repair. Mere Manor Youth Band took part in many regional and national contests from 1968 onwards and represented the West of England in both Youth and Fourth Section finals in London. The band played for many community events, gave concerts and had very successful tours in Holland, Germany and Luxembourg. In 1986 Adrienne and Bernard Howell retired from the band. Membership declined during

Nurse Wells with some of the babies she had delivered; a retirement party on Dewes House lawn, 1936.

Mere Infant Welfare Clinic party in the Lecture Hall, c.1967.

Right: *Mere Choral Society, c.1972. The conductor is Mrs Ada Hooper* (centre foreground) *and the pianist is Mrs Phyllis Cross.*

Below: *Miss Chafyn Grove's orchestra, c.1885.*

The Church of England Temperance Band in new uniforms, 1908. Left to right, back row: *Jim Deverill (tenor), Alec Coward (euphonium), Frank Sheppard (baritone), Lewis Sheppard (tenor), Reg Chaplin (trombone);* centre: *Bill Gray (cornet), George Gray (cornet), Fred Bristow (cornet), Jacob Gray (drums), Ted Hooper (bandmaster), Henry Chalke (clarinet);* front: *Jim Sheppard (E-flat bass), George Parfitt junr (cornet), Charlie Parfitt (tenor), George Parfitt senr (E-flat bass).*

Mere Town Silver Band, 1927.

the 1990s and the band stopped playing in 2000. Adrienne and Bernard have received 50-years'-service awards from the Wessex Brass Band Association. In 1964 the Howells founded the Mere Solo and Quartet Contest, attracting hundreds of entries from all over the country. It was held at the Duchy Manor School, then at Wincanton, and in 2004 is organised by Wincanton Town Band.

There has been, of course, a group of bell-ringers at the Parish Church for a very long time and at the time of writing there are still enthusiastic ringers, both men and women, who ring for Sunday services, weddings and special occasions. A handbell ringing group, Mere Melodies, was started in 1999 by Kathleen Herbert and her ringers have become very proficient; they have given performances at many local events. A complete two-octave set of new

Mere Town Silver Band, c.1960. Left to right, back row: David Antell, Jim Garrett, Tom Chaplin, Arthur Butt, Michael Gatehouse, George Maidment, Cyril Mills, Fred Tranter, Eric White; front: Ernie Suter, Jim Ford, Tim Burden, Derek Coward, Archie Ford, Billy Burt, Raymond Hill, Roger Gatehouse.

handbells was bought with the aid of a South Wiltshire Area Grant in 2002.

Mere Women's Institute was formed in 1918 and is one of the two oldest in Wiltshire. It started with 32 members paying an annual subscription of 2s. (ten pence in modern money) and by 1926 there were 101 members, some of them having joined in order to play tennis and hockey! Members have always looked beyond the monthly meeting, joining in county and national events and achieving success in a number of competitions. Their most notable success was in 1956 when their entry in a county competition to produce a village scrapbook was placed third. This was later used as the basis for the local history book *The Story of Mere*. The scrapbook is now held by Mere Museum. From 1943 and for a number of years thereafter members helped to organise a foot clinic in Mere and from 1959 they regularly helped in Mere Library. During the 1960s and 1970s there was a flourishing drama group whose most memorable productions were the popular pantomimes written by Alice Coward.

A branch of the YMCA was formed in 1869 but details of its history are unknown. In 1893 there was a Stour Vale branch of the Girls' Friendly Society and by 1910 there were 25 members from Mere. In 1930 Mere had its own branch of the GFS, which continued until about 1958. Its activities included handicrafts, singing and organised games.

After the First World War a club for the Comrades of the Great War was formed, becoming later the Wiltshire Regiment Old Comrades Association. A branch of the Royal British Legion was founded in

Above: *Mere Manor Youth Band led by Adrienne Howell, carnival day, September, 1984.*

Mere Manor Youth Band playing at Fives Court with Adrienne Howell conducting, 1985.

Bell-ringers at Mere Parish Church, c.1950. Left to right, back row: *Cecil Phillips, Percy Whitmarsh, Fred Green, Dave Milner, 'Copper' Coward, John Bunce;* front: *Harry Jordan, W. Keates, Jack Gray (captain), Jack Paul, Geoff Coward.*

Jack Gray, captain of the bells and keeper of the church clock, c.1980.

1921 and its clubhouse was erected in White Road on a piece of land acquired from the Duchy of Cornwall. The clubhouse was opened in 1923 by HRH The Prince of Wales. The Old Comrades Association shared this accommodation with the British Legion and after 1949 the annual parade and service of remembrance on Castle Hill in June or July was a joint effort by both organisations. A women's section of the British Legion was formed in 1935 for monthly meetings at the clubhouse and lasted until 1989. The men's section of the Legion closed in 1996 and its standard, with that of the women's section, is laid up in the Parish Church. (The colours of a regiment are 'laid up' when they are retired from active service.) The clubhouse continues to be used as the Prince of Wales Club.

The first troop of Boy Scouts in Mere was started as early as 1910. W.A. Norris was the first recorded scoutmaster and there is an early photograph showing an impressive number of boys in the troop and another picture shows a patrol camping at Ashwell. In 1923 the scoutmaster was Hubert Woodford with assistants Francis Alphin and Ralph Coward. Ewing Edmunds, the printer, was also scoutmaster at one time. At the time of writing there is still a flourishing Scout troop under Scout Leader Gary Edwards.

A Cub Scouts pack in Mere was first registered in 1925. Mrs Ann Ings was leader from 1959 to 1974 and then became Assistant District Commissioner (Cub Scouts) until 1995. She was awarded a Silver Acorn badge in 1987 for distinguished service to Scouting. Mrs Gladys Pope was a very successful Cub Scout leader during the 1970s. The leader at the time of writing is Mrs Jan Davis. There is a Beaver Colony

Past presidents of Mere Women's Institute at their diamond jubilee, 1978. Left to right, back row: *Mrs Webb, Mrs Mosse, Mrs Cassell, Mrs White, Mrs Pratt;* front: *Mrs A. Gray, Mrs N. Rutter, Mrs E. Gray, Miss J. Rutter, Mrs A.K. Hooper, Mrs J. Duckworth.*

Mere WI, 1954. Left to right, back row: Janet Coward, Alice Read, ?, Ada Hooper, Myfanwy Hooper; centre: *Mary Filor, Clarice Burden, Flo Burden, ?;* front: *Nell Burden, Jean Coward, Betty Coward, Frances Filor, ?.*

WI Show, Mere, October 1987. Left to right: Mrs J. Cole, Mrs J. Spiers, Mrs G. Pope, Mrs P. Durkee, Mrs M. White.

HRH The Prince of Wales meeting members of Mere Royal British Legion after opening their new clubhouse in 1923.

A parade of Royal British Legion members for the 43rd Wessex Division memorial service in Mere, June 1987.

of younger Scouts under the leadership of Mrs Caroline Edwards. Each section takes an active part in district events.

The first company of Girl Guides in Mere was started in 1926 by Miss Sithy Walton assisted by Daphne Hartgill (later Mrs Ralph Coward). Dorothy Durbin took over the company in 1932 and remained as captain until 1968. She was followed by Thelma Ings who led until 1981 when she received her Commissioner's warrant. The company has continued under several Guiders and has taken part in all county, division and district meetings. Many summer camps have been enjoyed over the years and a few lucky girls have been selected to join in Guiding events in Switzerland, Antigua and Nova Scotia. Quite a lot of members have qualified as Queen's Guides. The whole company contributes to community events. The organisation has seen changes to the uniform and to programmes of activities but continues to do well.

The first Mere Brownie pack was registered in 1927 with Mrs Ralph Coward as Brown Owl. She was followed by Miss Betty Coward. The pack has continued without a break to the present day. Sue Luffman and Sue Jeans are the leaders in 2004 and there is a waiting list for new entrants. The pack has done a lot of work for the community, such as planting flower-beds, entertaining at old people's homes and participating in the annual carnival. It has attended district and county events, including one at which HRH Princess Margaret and the Chief Guide were present and has had outdoor activity days, pack holidays and various expeditions.

At the time of writing there is also a Karate Club, taught and organised by Peter Manning and supported by an enthusiastic membership of boys, girls and adults.

In 1861 there was a Mere and Zeals Rifle Corps and then after the Second World War a Hinks Mill Home Guard Rifle Club was established. A British

Left: *Mere Scouts at a camp-fire, Ashwell, c.1915.*

Mere Scouts at their camp at Ashwell, c.1915

The Scout Hut in Dark Lane, 1980.

Mere Girl Guides, 1948. Left to right, back row: *Mary Hopkins, Gwen Welch, Susie Perrett, Pearl Lawley, Rita Avery, Janet White, Margaret Stone;* centre: *Janet Ayres, Tessa Wright, Ruth Ings, Brenda Symes, Pamela Cherbury, Pauline Edmonds, Rosemary Pinnigar, Jean Welch;* front: *Jennifer Hole, Janet Long, Mary Habgood, Dorothy Durbin (captain), Thelma Ford, Pat Habgood, Damaris Johnson.*

Cub Scouts in Mere, 1987. Left to right: *James Brown, Jake Doddington, Peter Read, Luke Jonas, David Read, John Durkee, Lee Haskett, Peter Burden.*

Mere Cub Scouts at camp in Zeals Park, 1949. Left to right, back row: *Elaine Bryant, Dorothy George, Clarice Burden;* third row: *Alan Deverill, Spencer Pearce, Alan Lawrence, Richard Gatehouse;* second row: *Anthony Warren, Michael Norris, Freddie Mills, Brian Hill, Bevan Bird, Brian Ings, John Hopkins, Michael Burden;* front: *Barry Gray, Michael Mills, Brian Perrett, Derek Stone, Eric Coward.*

Mere Brownies and Guides, 1950s.

Mere Brownies and Guides at a Thinking Day service at Mere Parish Church, 1976.

Mere Guides and Brownies tree planting in Castle Hill Approach in the 1960s.

Legion Small Bore Rifle Club was also formed in 1934. A detachment of the Army Cadet Force was set up in Mere in about 1950 and, under Captain Howarth, Captain Martin and Lt Dence, lasted until about 1970. Meetings were held at their hut in Angel Lane and the unit took part in annual camps, shooting competitions, sports and parades.

There was a Castle Hill Lodge of the RAOB (Royal Antidiluvian Order of Buffaloes) active in Mere in the 1950s and 1960s. The date of its inception is unknown.

From 1948 until the 1960s barber Vic Humphries and his wife organised an annual outing to Weymouth for the old folk of the town. The costs were met by donations in a house-to-house collection and the excursions by coach were very popular. Several photographs of these outings are held by Mere Museum.

The White Tudor Club for older Mere residents started in 1962 under the chairmanship of Mrs Christine Wallis in Miss Sylvia Whyte's Tudor Tea Rooms in Church Street. The club chose its name in recognition of Miss Whyte's generosity in accommodating them every Wednesday afternoon and for providing tea and entertainment. The club continues in 2004, meeting in the Grove Buildings. A day centre at the Lynch Close residents' communal room (staffed by volunteers) offers a cooked midday meal on two days a week to a number of elderly people and they enjoy an afternoon of entertainment followed by tea. If required, transport for attenders is provided by voluntary drivers.

Mere Rifle Club c.1960. Left to right, back row: *Ken Deverill, Hubert Sheppard, Dennis Gould, Ron Ball;* front: *'Farmer' Brain, Bill Burden, Chris Elford.*

Mere Army Cadet Corps parading in Church Street, c.1955.

Mere Old Folks' Tea, 1 July 1959. *The event was arranged by Mr Vic Humphries* (seated in the front row, fourth from the right).

The opening of Mere Bowls Club's new pavilion. The chairman of Salisbury District Council, Mrs Errington-Rycroft, makes the opening bowl.

Right: *Gideon Burden bowling at Walter Burden's bowling-green, c.1950. Frank Ford is standing.*

Mere Football Club, 1897–99. Left to right, standing: G. Cope, G. Herrington, E. Gray, E. Eastwood, W. Taylor, B. Mitchell, R. Henslow; sitting: F. Rutter, W. Pitman, J. Fricker, P. Norman, F. Sharpe.

The Mere Snooker Club was founded in 1922 in the former Liberal Club in Salisbury Street. A condition of membership was – and still is – that no alcohol should be consumed on the premises. The club has two snooker tables and has a small but enthusiastic membership.

The records of Mere Tennis Club date back to 1925 when land in Pettridge Lane (next to Greystones) was acquired and two grass courts laid. In 1960 these courts were sold and play continued in the grounds of Dewes House until 1962 when two new hard tennis-courts were made in the recreation-ground. A pavilion was then bought from Wincanton Tennis Club but replaced by the present one in 1973. The season commences in April although the courts are available through the winter months for any member who wishes to play. At the time of writing there are around 30 members. In 1930, as remembered by Mr John Burden, there were 13 other privately-owned tennis-courts in Mere which keen players might use.

Mere Badminton Club had minutes dating back to 1952 but the club probably existed before that. It played at the Victoria Hall until about 1963 then transferred to the Duchy Manor School until 1983. Subsequently, courts at Port Regis School, Motcombe, were hired. The club was successful in many competitions but, unfortunately, membership declined and the club closed in 1997.

Mere Bowls Club originally played on a private green in the garden of Mr Walter Burden's house, The Yews, in North Road. After Mr Burden's death his son Roy invited his bowling friends to form a club to be called the Burden (Mere) Bowling Club in memory of his father. When Roy Burden left Mere in 1974 Salisbury District Council purchased The Yews property for housing development but agreed to lease the bowling-green to the club. This arrangement still holds at the time of writing. The original picturesque rustic pavilion had deteriorated dangerously by 1991 so with the help of grants, a new pavilion was built in 1992. Since then, members have carried out further improvements to the pavilion and the green. The club has a keen membership of some 30 men and women and plays about 30 friendly matches in a season.

There was a late-nineteenth century football club which played on a pitch in Pettridge Lane. When the recreation-ground was created during the 1920s the club had two pitches there. In the 1925/26 season it had great success as winners in the Shaftesbury District League, in the Wincanton District League and for the Shaftesbury Charity cup. There is no active football club in 2004.

A Mere United Cricket Club was formed in 1867 with practices held alternately at Zeals Park and Barrow Street Farm. The present Mere Cricket Club plays at Mere's recreation-ground where it had a pavilion until a fire destroyed it in 2002.

In 1983 the Mere Allotment Holders' and Leisure Gardeners' Society was renamed Mere Horticultural Society and continued under that name until 2003 when it became Mere Gardening Society. In addition to a wide-ranging programme of speakers on gardening matters the society stages a popular Vegetable, Fruit and Flower Show each year. The Mere (St Michael's) Chrysanthemum Society held annual

Mere Football Club, 1924–25. Left to right, back row: G. Francis, L. Gray, H. Bristow, J. Whitmarsh, P. Cosgrove; centre: A. Parker, B. Woodford, A. Ford; front: ? Maidment, J. Coward, D. Hooper, G. White, H. Cowley.

Mere Football Club, 1948–49. Left to right, back row: *George Francis, Dick Avery, Bob Shave, Douglas Lawley, Frank Ford;* centre: *Alf Jukes, George Thomas, Bill Newcombe, Tom Newcombe (trainer);* front: *Don Graham, Wilf Stobbs, Phil Avery, Pat Austin, Hubert Hooper.*

Mere Football Club, 1983. Left to right, back row: *Michael Bray, ?, Chris Hussey, Timothy Cowley, ?, John Howell;* front: *Peter Davie, Neville Francis, Ian Brockway, Steve Howell, Graham Starr.*

Mere Cricket Club, mid-1930s. Left to right, back row: ?, J. Avery, R. Dovey, Revd Wearne, ?, F. Stone, W. Lidbury; centre: *E. Brice, G. Yeoman, G. White;* front: *F. Ford, S. Riddick, A. Stainer, C. Lawrence.*

Trophy winners at Mere Horticultural Society Show, 1987. Left to right: E. Laman, J. Walsh, P. Rossi, R. Smith, L. Yale, Mrs S. Farrington (who presented the trophies), Y. Chandler, J. Joyce, A. Chislett, D. Potter.

The Mere (St Michael's) Chrysanthemum Society Show, c.1960. Left to right: Kitty Taylor, Mrs Bennett, Revd N. Johnson, ?, Frank Stone, Mary Gething. The children in the picture have not been identified.

Chrysanthemum, Fruit and Produce Shows at the Lecture Hall from 1949 for more than 20 years, organised by Mrs Kitty Taylor and Miss Mary Gething.

The Gillingham, Mere and Shaftesbury Lions Club was chartered in 1979 starting with four members from Mere. The total membership at the time of writing is 18 and includes a few women. There are two meetings each month held at Milton on Stour. The club supports many good causes in the district and there is a tradition of bringing a Father Christmas float to Mere every December to raise funds; its arrival in the town is eagerly anticipated by both adults and children alike.

A Mere branch of the Workers' Educational Association came into being in 1939. The WEA was founded as a national organisation in 1903 to promote the higher education of working people. In Mere, the group started with 22 members and around this number attend in 2004 with a programme of two courses a year given at the Lecture Hall. The courses have wide appeal, varying between such subjects as music appreciation and computer skills. The founding secretary and treasurer was Joyce Rutter and she served for many years. The chairman in 2004 is Mrs Margaret Durkee.

In 1946 a Youth Centre was set up at The Gables, Salisbury Street (Gilyard Scarth's office in 2004) rented from the Lecture Hall Trust and sponsored by the Local Youth Service Council. A resident warden was employed and the property included a large games room and several smaller rooms as well as the flat for the warden. For the first few years it was very successful and met the needs of the town but by 1953 it lost support and closed down. A Youth Club was revived in the 1960s and during the 1970s a building for the club was put up in the recreation-ground. This still serves as the Mere Youth Development Centre with meetings held twice a week for young people aged 12–18. At Barrow Street Farm near West Knoyle the Barn Buddies was started at the beginning of the twenty-first century and under the sound leadership of Tim and Mary Merrell has been very successful with an average attendance of 30 boys and girls over seven years of age.

A Red Cross detachment was very active in Mere during the First World War, when a hospital run by the organisation operated in the Grove Buildings. The detachment survived in some form through to the Second World War when it organised various sales to raise money for the war effort. In 1973 a British Red Cross Society ambulance was purchased as a result of hard work by many local people and it was stationed at the old fire station in The Square. It was used to supplement the County Ambulance Service in emergencies and it provided first-aid facilities for many local events including the Fêtes Champêtre at Stourhead. There is no longer an ambulance stationed in Mere but the detachment still provides a service for outdoor events and gives cover for the matches played at the North Dorset Rugby Club. It also has a medical aid loan service and

Mere WEA members celebrating the centenary of the Association at Stourhead, May 2003.

Members of Mere Youth Club in the garden of Dewes House, c.1946.

Members of Mere Youth Club, c.1961.

British Red Cross Society, Bourton, Silton and Mere Detachments at Zeals, c.1914.

British Red Cross Society, Mere Detachment sale in the Lecture Hall, c.1950.

organises courses in first aid. There is a week in May each year when house-to-house collections are made for the society and most of the town is covered by volunteer collectors.

A Mere branch of the Cancer Research Campaign, now Cancer Research UK, was formed in 1974 on the initiative of the vicar, the Revd Raymond Preston Thomas. Annual sales and jumble sales have been arranged and in 1985 the annual sale became a May Fayre. This is now a major event for Mere each summer and large crowds attend the many stalls set up in and around The Square. The total amount raised for the charity by the Mere branch has now topped £200,000 – a magnificent result. In 2001 awards for 25 years' service were given to Mrs Dorothy George, Mr Brian James and Mrs Evelyn Frampton and for 10 years' service to Mr and Mrs Derek Wilson.

As a means of promoting better co-operation and understanding between the churches in and around Mere, a Mere and District Council of Churches (now Churches Together in Mere and District) organisation was proposed by the vicar, the Revd John Smith who acted as its first chairman. Combined services have been held in the participating churches, various joint meetings arranged and on every Good Friday there is a procession of witness from The Square to the summit of Castle Hill. More than 100 people are usually in the procession, a large wooden cross is carried by a succession of volunteers, prayers and meditations are read at intervals on the journey and the cross is finally erected on the summit of the hill where it stays for three days.

The late Mrs Ursula Flanaghan of Deans Orchard suggested that a Friends of St Michael the Archangel Church group should be formed to provide funding for those improvements to the Parish Church that might be outside the responsibility of the Parochial Church Council. It was inaugurated in 1977 and she acted as its first secretary. The Friends have continued under a succession of vicars as chairmen and a lot has been done to beautify the church and pay for restoration. The north-west corner of the church is now designated as the Friends' Corner where a fine new set of shelves and cupboards has recently been installed. Various events are organised by the Friends to raise money and it is supported by members in many parts of this country and abroad.

There is a Friends of Mere Museum group which raises money for the local museum by having one springtime and one autumn event and by subscriptions and donations. The group runs a small sales desk in the museum and in 1994 sponsored the production of a coloured pictorial map of Mere designed and drawn by Dr Colin Anderson. The map is now an outstanding exhibit in the museum. The Friends also contributed to the financing of four large panels describing 'Mere in the Twentieth Century' which have been put on display as a Millennium Project by the museum.

Mere Historical Society was founded in 1972 at the suggestion of Mrs Christine Wallis who was a member of the Local History Committee that had produced the book *The Story of Mere*. An inaugural meeting was held in the library and about 30 people signed up as founder members. Mrs Wallis was elected secretary and it was largely due to her enthusiasm and efficiency that the society became so successful, having four lectures in the winter months and four outings in the summer. The society now has a membership of about 200 and attracts people not only from Mere but from surrounding villages too.

In 1966 a Mere Oxfam Group was started and Christine Wallis acted as its secretary. Various fundraising events were organised and after 1969 there was an Oxfam shop which at first opened annually in October and then, in later years, twice a year. The group wound up in 1997 and after 31 years a total of nearly £40,000 had been raised for the cause. Gilbert Harris was its treasurer between 1966 and 1983 and Judy Bickerstaff succeeded him. Andy Bickerstaff was its last chairman. A pledged gift scheme for Oxfam has continued, raising over £400 a year, thanks to the hard work of collecting done by Barbara Naylor.

Mere Cancer Research Campaign sale in the Lecture Hall, c.1966. Left to right: *Dorothy George, Bill Walworth, Revd Raymond Preston Thomas, Eileen Paul.*

Mere Cancer Research Campaign May Fayre held in The Square, 14 May 1988.

Above: *Good Friday procession of witness on Castle Hill, 1986.*

Mere Cancer Research Campaign; long-service award winners, 2001. Left to right, back row: *Mrs A. Wilson, Mr D. Wilson, ?, Dr D. Longbourne;* front: *Mr B. James, Mrs D. George, Mrs E. Frampton.*

Dr Colin Anderson and the map he produced for Mere Museum in 1994. The photograph was taken for the Village of the Year Competition, 2000.

The unveiling of the Millennium Panels 'Mere in the Twentieth Century' in Mere Museum, December 1999. Left to right: Mrs Norah Rutter, Dr David Longbourne, Dr Colin Anderson, Mr Michael Tighe, Mr Bill Hayter.

Mrs Christine Wallis on her retirement after 20 years as secretary of Mere Historical Society, March 1992.

The first Oxfam shop in Mere, 1970. Left to right: Mr J. Paul, Mrs M. Airey, Mrs N. Rutter, Mrs C. Wallis, Mr G. Harris, Miss J. Rutter.

In 1989, initiated by Parish Councillor Michael Taylor, a Mere Footpath Group was formed to improve the parish footpaths. A programme of clearing footpaths, building stiles and bridges, and putting up waymarks was started. Extensive restoration of the old sheep wash and mill-wheel at Burton was undertaken. Altogether, 70 stiles, and three bridges were repaired and most of the footpaths cleared and waymarked. In 1990 the group was given a certificate of merit in the Wiltshire Village Venture Competition and in 1991 it received an award of £1,000 from the British Trust for Conservation Volunteers, sponsored by Esso. The repairing work is in abeyance at the time of writing but the group continues to organise walks in and around the district.

A Mere and District Linkscheme was launched in January 1996 under the chairmanship of the vicar, the Revd Ben Elliott. It offers a care service to the elderly, sick, disabled or housebound and a transport service for people needing help in getting to hospital and to doctors' surgeries, etc., made possible by the use of 35 or more voluntary car drivers. Those receiving these services are asked to make donations and the scheme has been partly funded in this way as well as by local authority grants. However, a major contributor to the scheme is the Mere Literary Festival held each October and organised by Adrienne Howell. The festival has not only been a great success in its own right but has raised several thousand pounds for the Linkscheme.

A number of charities are supported by volunteers arranging sales, flag days or making house-to-house collections. These include the RNLI, NSPCC, RSPCA, Earl Haig Fund, Age Concern, and Marie Curie Cancer Care.

Most clubs and societies have fortunes that wax and wane and some do not survive when membership falls. However, generally speaking Mere's voluntary organisations are alive and well and there can be few people here who can say that this town has nothing to offer them for their hobbies and pastimes.

Members of Mere Footpath Group, 1990.

A meet of the South & West Wilts Hunt in The Square, early-twentieth century.

A meet of the South & West Wilts Hunt in Angel Lane, c.1955.

Chapter 13

The Twentieth and Twenty-First Centuries

Many events in Mere's twentieth- and twenty-first-century schools, churches, houses, trades and voluntary organisations have already been discussed in previous chapters. As in most towns and villages there have been huge changes brought about by the motor car, telephone, radio, television, and computer, with improvements in public health and public services.

Mere is no longer the isolated rural community that it was at the beginning of the twentieth century. It was then largely self-sufficient in food production and in having shops to supply all needs. Socially it was close-knit, with marriage between local families being common and often resulting in large families of children. There was much prejudiced feeling between 'church' and 'chapel' and between supporters of differing political parties. Most of these narrow views have, fortunately, largely disappeared.

The two world wars made an enormous difference to the town. Troops billeted or stationed in Mere brought new ideas and challenges to this small country town and those Mere-born ex-servicemen who returned home had a wider knowledge of the world outside their hometown.

At the beginning of the First World War, men of the Royal Artillery were billeted in Mere, some at the Temperance Hotel where there was stabling for their horses. Their training was done on the downs with horses pulling the gun carriages. A house near the Talbot Garage in Salisbury Street and another at The Triangle were used as guard rooms. The Grove Buildings were turned into a Red Cross Hospital and casualties were received direct from the Front. A total of 1,273 sick and wounded soldiers were treated here. Mrs Arthur White was the commandant and Dr Farnfield was medical officer. A wooden plaque now

Mounted Royal Field Artillery, Mere, 1914.

Royal Artillery soldiers billeted at Mere, 1914.

139

Above: *Reservists from Mere during the First World War.*

Right: *The Red Cross Hospital in the Grove Buildings, 1914–19.*

Red Cross nurses and patients at the Grove Buildings, 1914–19.

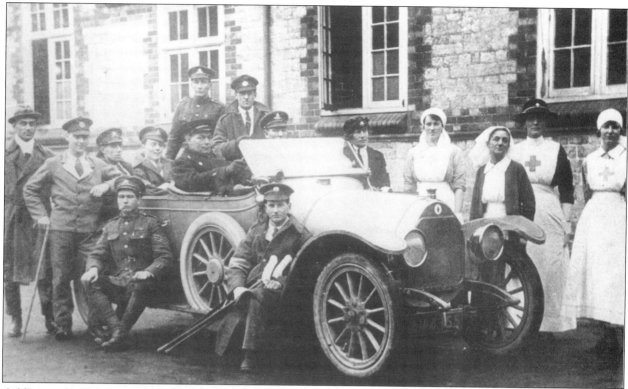

Soldiers and nurses from the Red Cross Hospital, Mere, with Lady Hoare's car.

A commemorative panel for the Red Cross Hospital in the Grove Buildings.

in the Grove Buildings records the names of 74 people who helped as nurses and orderlies in the hospital from October 1914 to February 1919. The Lecture Hall became a 'Tipperary Club' for the troops. After the war a war memorial was put up in The Square and the 46 names of the fallen were engraved on it. These names were also inscribed in a book of remembrance in the Parish Church.

At the start of the Second World War, men of the Royal Corps of Signals were billeted in Mere. A camp was built in Manor Road and men from the Grenadier Guards, the Coldstream Guards, Military Police and American Army (the 3rd Armoured Division) were in turn stationed there. In October 1945, Polish troops of the 5th Division and 14th Brigade who had fought at Monte Casino in the Italian campaign came to the Manor Road camp and stayed until early 1947. A canteen was organised at The Triangle and a quiet room arranged for reading and writing at the Methodist schoolroom behind the chapel. The Lecture Hall was requisitioned and used for a variety of purposes.

Mere had a Home Guard unit and ARP wardens had their headquarters at the Toc-H Hall behind the Old Ship Hotel. In 1942 an airfield opened at Zeals where Spitfires and Hurricanes were based. It was later used by the US Airforce, as well as Canadian and New Zealand squadrons. In 1944 the airfield was used as a glider training school then in 1945/46 it was taken over by the Admiralty and closed down early in 1946. In July 1940 a German Heinkel 111 crashed at Huntingford, killing all the crew. In October 1940 a Hurricane was shot down, crashing at

The war memorial in The Square.

memorial in The Square and to the book of remembrance in the Parish Church. A Welcome Home Fund was collected and distributed to Mere men who returned after service. On 21 May 1949 a memorial to the 43rd Wessex Division was unveiled on the summit of Castle Hill. It is a replica of the memorial on Hill 112 near Caen, Normandy, which marks the site of the first major battle for the Division in July 1944. A service of remembrance is held on Castle Hill every year for old comrades of the Division.

During the First World War Mrs Alice Rutter, wife of the Mere doctor, opened The Retreat, a home for unmarried mothers, in the building in Salisbury Street now occupied by Gilyard Scarth, estate agents. Mrs Rutter was honorary superintendent and Dr Rutter honorary treasurer and medical officer. A matron and deputy matron were employed. In 1919 the home was enlarged by extension into two adjacent cottages. Over the ten years of its existence, over 300 girls were admitted. Residence would normally be for six months and the societies or individuals nominating the girls for admission paid 10s. a week and 1 guinea on confinement. Whenever possible, arrangements were made for the babies to remain with their mothers but some fosterings and adoptions were found to be necessary. It must have taken

Wellhead, the pilot surviving with severe burns. In March 1941 a German bomber crashed near Kingston Deverill and in July that year a British bomber crashed at Lower Mere Park Farm. On 10 July 1944, a Mosquito overshot Zeals airfield and crashed at Penselwood, the two crewmen surviving. On the same day, which was foggy, a USAAF Norseman was refused permission to land at Zeals and struck the top of Alfred's Tower, killing all on board. On 19 February 1945, a Dakota crashed at Beech Knoll, Stourton, soon after taking off from Zeals, killing everyone on board. A gap in the trees on the knoll caused by the crash is still visible and a memorial on the site was unveiled in 1995.

Mere fire brigade gave magnificent war service between 1939 and 1945, fighting fires in Bath, Bristol and elsewhere.

Great efforts were made in Mere and district during the special Savings Weeks held during the Second World War. For example, in 1942 there was a Warship Week and a shield-shaped plaque, now in Mere Museum, commemorates the adoption by Mere and district of the minesweeper HMS *Kingston Agate*. In 1943 there was a Wings for Victory Week and in 1944 a Salute the Soldier Week and for each of these, Mere received a commemorative plaque.

After the war, the names of the 12 local men who had died for their country were added to the war

The memorial to the crew of the Dakota that crashed at Beech Knoll, Stourton, on 19 February 1945, killing all on board. The gap in the trees marks the path of the ill-fated aircraft.

Mere Home Guard unit, c.1940. Left to right, back row: *P. Flower, C. Whitmarsh, ?;* third row: *R. Shave, W. Lawrence, W. Gray, G. Pester, R. Sims, R. Bourton;* second row: *T. Burfitt, A. Warre, F. Bristow, W. Mills, E. Horrell, R. Doddington, H. Abraham;* front: *R. Warren, A. Coward, R. Stratton, ?, L. Vincent.*

Mere fire brigade, 1943–44.

Mere fire brigade, 1955. Left to right, back row: *R. Sheppard, C. Deverill, D. Bristow, F. Curtis, F. Hirst;* front: *M. Sheppard, L. Brady, A. Ford, S. Templeman, W. Young.*

Mrs Alice Rutter and some of the babies at The Retreat, c.1920.

The 43rd Wessex Division war memorial on Castle Hill.

Dr Francis B. Rutter, c.1930.

considerable courage for Dr and Mrs Rutter to have launched this venture at a time when illegitimacy was so frowned upon in 'respectable circles' and in a small community such as Mere. When Dr Rutter died in 1932 his work for The Retreat was rightly described in a memorial tribute as 'a splendid rescue work of quite unique quality'.

Dr Rutter had retired from practice in 1926 and Dr Elliot Whitby succeeded him at Dewes House. Dr Owen Hart came as assistant to Dr Whitby in 1938 and, after serving in the RAMC during the Second World War, returned as a partner in 1947, practising from his house, St Ann's in Church Street. The National Health Service was introduced in 1948 and medical practice in Mere and elsewhere was suddenly very different for doctors and patients. Dr Whitby retired in 1958 and Dr Hart retired in 1961 when author Dr Longbourne succeeded him. The doctor's surgery was, from 1964 to 1990, at The Old Rectory, Church Street. Dr Price came to Mere in 1987 and Dr McBride in 1990 when Dr Longbourne retired and a new surgery was built in Dark Lane. Dr Andrews joined as a partner in 2003.

In 1976 a purpose-built home for the elderly was opened by the local authority in Angel Lane and named Fives Court (because of the old fives court wall that stands nearby). It has provided a way of keeping the old and frail of Mere in familiar surroundings and the care of the 30 or so residents is of a high standard. It is now owned by the Order of St John Care Trust. A privately owned home for the elderly accommodating about 32 residents is at Bramley House, Castle Street.

In 1907 it was estimated that 150 houses in Mere and district had been allowed to fall into decay and a large number of these belonged to the Duchy of

Fives Court, Angel Lane, 1976.

Cornwall. The Duchy preferred to lease land to the larger farmers to save the cost of administration. Consequently, the small farmers found it almost impossible to get land. The need was met in part by the Mere and District Smallholders' Association set up by Dr Rutter and Mr Arthur White in 1908 with Mr Walter Burden as secretary. The first farm to be taken over was Burton Farm. This farm and others were split into smallholdings and by 1923 40 small-holders were renting a total of nearly 2,000 acres. The scheme was a great success and was one means of resettling men returning to Mere after the First World War. Control of the association was eventually handed to the County Smallholdings Committee.

Some 80 acres of Duchy land were at one time let to the parish for allotments at Burton Field, Southbrook, White Road and North Road. In the past, such allotments were eagerly sought after; sadly now there are fewer tenants with plots at Southbrook, North Road and Jack Paul Close.

Mere smallholders, 1909.

During the Second World War the farmers were called upon to double production from the land and many green fields were ploughed up to grow potatoes and corn. The combine harvester was introduced to many farms towards the end of the war and, with the installation of electricity on farms, the milking machine also became a common aid to farmers. German and Italian prisoners of war were available for farm work and in 1941 a Women's Land Army hostel was opened at Southbrook with about 20 young women allocated to carry out field and dairy work.

In 1908 two wells were sunk at Burton Field and by 1909 Mere had a piped water-supply for the first time. The Prince and Princess of Wales (later King George V and Queen Mary) came to Mere on 24 July 1909 to officially open the new waterworks by pulling a scarlet cord attached to a fire hose in The Square. A jet of water splashed people who had crowded too close but the royal couple escaped a soaking! In 1914 a reservoir was built in Warminster Hollow which was sufficient to supply Gillingham and Shaftesbury as well as Mere. In 1947 two more deep wells were sunk at Burton Field producing up to a million gallons per day. In 1951 an additional reservoir was built a little above the existing one and in 1954 a new pumping station was installed over the two deep wells. In 1965/66 another reservoir was completed on Whitesheet Hill and a second one on

that site was made in 1995. A replacement for the first reservoir in Warminster Hollow was constructed and the pumping station renovated in 1997.

Mere's first refuse collection started in about 1930, performed by a contractor at three-month intervals. In 1946 a monthly collection was arranged by the Rural District Council who changed it to a fortnightly collection in 1953. There is now a weekly collection of rubbish – now mostly in black plastic bags, not dustbins – and a fortnightly collection of waste paper with a 'special collection' service for large items which can be booked through the Mere Information Point. Bins for collecting bottles, cans and paper for recycling are available in the town car park.

In 1912 the Prince of Wales (later King Edward VIII) visited Duchy-owned farms in Mere. He returned in 1923 to meet his tenants and to inspect members of the Mere British Legion who paraded by their new clubhouse in White Road. Members of the Mere Detachment of the British Red Cross Society were also presented. He came to the town again in 1932 and visited Mr Walter Burden's nurseries at Burton Field. He lunched at the Old Ship Hotel and left by aeroplane from Mere Down. In 1942 King George VI and Queen Elizabeth came to the Manor Road camp to present new colours to the King's Company, Grenadier Guards, stationed there. On 3 July 1952, Queen Elizabeth II visited Mere. As a result of an outbreak of foot-and-mouth disease on local

Members of the Women's Land Army outside their hostel at Southbrook, Mere, during the Second World War.

Above: *Samuel Lander with a drilling rig in Burton Field shortly before water was struck there in 1908.*

Above: *The first water reservoir for Mere and Gillingham in Warminster Hollow, 1914.*

Building the reservoir at White-sheet, 1965–66.

Building a new reservoir in Warminster Hollow, 1996–97.

Above: *HRH The Prince of Wales meeting the Mere British Red Cross Detachment in 1923. He is speaking to Mrs Arthur White, the commandant.*

The visit to Mere by HM Queen Elizabeth II on 3 July 1952. On her right is Mr Alan Coward, chairman of Mere Parish Council.

Prince Charles leaving St Michael's Church during his visit to Mere, 17 May 1979. The vicar of Mere was then Revd John Smith.

farms she could not visit any Duchy farms here so instead met her tenants at the Hill Brush Company's factory. At the recreation-ground a great crowd of children greeted her before she went to see the green-houses at Burton Field where Her Majesty was presented with a spray of orchids grown by Mr Walter Burden. In 1970 Prince Charles met Duchy tenants at Manor Farm and when he came again in 1979 he was given a tour of the Parish Church where he 'signed in' as the first member of the Friends of St Michael's.

In 1920 it was suggested to the Parish Council that a memorial to the First World War – a 'Peace Memorial' – should take the form of a recreation-ground for Mere. A committee was formed to look into the matter under the chairmanship of Dr Rutter and, after negotiating with the Duchy of Cornwall, a piece of land at Burton Field was bought, the costs being met by public subscription, by organising a Peace Memorial Fête and from grants, including one from the Carnegie Trust. The Peace Memorial Committee handed over control of the recreation-ground to the Parish Council in 1931 and the council still maintains it. After Dr Rutter's death the parish raised a further £400 to provide a pavilion on the site – the Rutter Pavilion – in his memory but this was not opened until 1933. A good selection of play equipment for young children in the recreation-ground has been provided over the years by the Parish Council. In addition it has provided more equipment in a fenced-off area at the foot of Castle Hill for a similar playground.

In 1924 Dr Rutter founded and endowed the Lecture Hall Trust, which aimed to promote the welfare of Mere people 'along lines not inconsistent with Nonconformist Christianity, Temperance or similar objects'. The management of the Lecture Hall was entrusted to a large number of trustees and in 1928 the Small Lecture Hall was added to the building and was used for many years as a Friends' (Quakers') Meeting House. The hall is also used for a wide variety of meetings, sales and entertainments and it is where the Parish Council holds its monthly meetings open to the public.

In 1927 the first County Branch Library opened in a small room in the former Junior School in Boar Street. In 1947 it was moved to the Liberal Club

Mere recreation-ground, 1979.

The first County Library in Mere, at Boar Street, 1927.

premises in Salisbury Street and then in May 1970, to the old National School in Church Street. Space in the new library was given to the Local History Committee (later to become Mere Historical Society) to have four showcases for a museum of local history. The management of this museum later came under an independent Mere Museum Committee which appointed an honorary curator. The author, Dr Longbourne, has performed the role of curator since 1984 and, with help from many quarters, the stock of artefacts, photographs and documents (including those from the former Church Museum) has increased and the number of display cases doubled. The museum has excellent support from the town

and from the County Museums Service. It has won two awards, one from the Gulbenkian Foundation in 1998 and another from the South West Museums Council in 1999. Dr Jenny Wilding was appointed honorary assistant curator in 2001. Mere Museum continues to have displays on a variety of local historical subjects which change every three months and maintains a computerised catalogue index of its collection for reference and research.

Mere's annual carnival was first held in 1928 and from 1932 there has been an almost unbroken series of carnival queens chosen each year to lead the festivities. The carnival, usually held in September, lasts a week and events organised by a carnival committee

Mere Library and Museum housed in the former National School, Church Street, since 1970.

Mere Museum, July 2002.

Mere Carnival, 1932. The carnival queen was Mrs Joan White.

Mere Carnival, 1956. The carnival queen was Penny Hargreaves.

A Mere Carnival float, date unknown.

The Congregational Church Young People's Fellowship float, 1954. Left to right: *Jean Long, Sylvia Mills, ?, Catherine Bristow, Richard Long, David Bristow, Christopher Coward.*

include dances, plays, a baby show and fancy-dress competitions. A visiting fair comes for the final three nights of the week. The highlight of the event is a grand procession through the town for which a number of cups and trophies are awarded for the best carnival floats. The money raised from each carnival is shared out between chosen local organisations and good causes.

In 1984 the vicar of Mere, the Revd Ben Elliott, initiated a new 'town' magazine to replace the church magazines that, until that time, had been published each month. He named it 'Mere Matters and so does West Knoyle' with a front cover showing a bird's-eye view of Mere drawn by Mr Tom O'Connor. The free magazine has continued to be issued on a monthly basis ever since, supported by advertising and donations. It has been a great success, now under the editorship of John Wilson (who provides a variety of cover pictures). The magazine has proved to be a popular and useful means for the many voluntary organisations and the Parish Council to advertise and record events, as well as for residents to be kept informed about what is going on in Mere and West Knoyle. The excellent *Blackmore Vale Magazine* published in Stalbridge as a free weekly magazine, edited by Fanny Charles, a former resident of Mere, is also a good way of keeping up with local news and views and it has a wide readership. The *Western Gazette*, published at Yeovil and the *Salisbury Journal*

are both well-patronised local newspapers.

With an increasing volume of traffic using the A303 which passed through Mere it was decided in 1962 to remove a bottleneck at the western end of Salisbury Street by demolishing the old Tudor house (The Triangle). As a further measure, a bypass for Mere was built and opened in 1975 thus relieving the town centre of much traffic. However, this move caused concern to those shopkeepers who relied upon tourists and other passing trade. There is still an ongoing problem with cars and lorries coming through Mere as well as with parking but this is a difficulty shared by most other towns and villages in the country.

At the end of the twentieth century and into the twenty-first century there are fewer 'Mere born' (with nice Wiltshire accents) and more 'incomers' who, happily, have become integrated into the community. Mere has a justified reputation for supporting good causes and for the strength of good feeling between the local churches. There is a wide selection of work in and within easy reach of Mere and little poverty. It is surrounded by beautiful countryside and is a very fine place in which to live. In 1967, 1992 and 1997 Mere won awards in the Best Kept Village competition organised by the CPRE and in 2000 was a runner up in a 'Great Britain Village of the Year' competition. Mere people have a real affection for and are proud of their town and may it be so for many years to come.

Mere bypass in 1979.

Left: *Cup winners in a children's fancy-dress parade, Mere Carnival, late-twentieth century.*

A Festival of Britain Pageant at The Chantry, 1951.

A general view of Mere from the church tower, 1978.

Index

Subscribers

Carol Adams (née Dennett), Gillingham, Dorset

Richard P. and Rosemary A. Adams, Mere, Wiltshire

Mrs Sue E. Adams, Mere, Wiltshire

Roger Adcock, Loxbeare, Devon

Mrs Lynn Allen, Mere, Wiltshire

Dr Colin Anderson, Mere, Wiltshire

Neil C. Anderson, Hillingdon, Middlesex

Eileen Anderton (formerly Chaffin)

John Archer and Family, Agonac, formerly Mere

Glenys Austin, Mere

Ben Avery, Mere, Wiltshire

Derrick and Sheila Avery, Victoria, Australia

Ernest F.E. (Eddie) Avery, Mere, Wiltshire

Lynda K. Avery, Mere, Wiltshire

Michael J. Avery, Mere, Wiltshire

Rita Bardwell, Mere

Randolph Steven James Berry, Mere, Wiltshire

Martin and Sharon Bielby, Bishop's Stortford, Hertfordshire

Audrey and Dennis Bignell, Bridgetown, Somerset

Margot Bird, Mere, Wiltshire

Andrew Bristow, Mere, Wiltshire

David Bristow, Bourton, Dorset

Derek and Joan Bristow, Mere, Wiltshire

Duncan Bristow, Mere, Wiltshire

Garry and Tina Bristow, Marple Bridge, Cheshire

Mr H.R. Bristow, Maidstone, Kent

Lucy Bristow, Salisbury, Wiltshire

Mr R.M. Brown, Mere, Wiltshire

Christopher G. Bubb

Gary and Jackie Burns, Calgary, Canada

Stephen and Valerie Burroughs, Mere, Wiltshire

Jack and Trudi Burton (née Riddick), Oak Lodge, Rownhams, Hampshire

Peter L. Button, Mere, Wiltshire

Lieutenant Colonel and Mrs Philip Carter

Julian Cassell, Sherborne, Dorset

Louise Cassell, Bristol

Robin Cassell, Motcombe, Dorset

Sonja Cassell (née Zinkova), formerly of Mere

David Chalke, Mere, Wiltshire

James Chalke, Gillingham, Dorset

Dr John Chandler, East Knoyle

Douglas and Angela Chislett, Mere, Wiltshire

Tony and Pam Clarke, The George Inn

Anthony Claydon, East Knoyle, Wiltshire

Rev and Mrs David Collinson, Shilbottle

Mr Norman Cooper, Mere, Wiltshire

Antony and Samantha Cotton, Mere, Wiltshire

Andrew Coward, Greenwich, London

Charles Coward, Chelsea, London

Clare Coward, Sherborne, Dorset

Colin Alan Coward, Mere, Wiltshire

David and Janet Coward, Mere, Wiltshire

Jean M. Coward (née Welch), Mere

Martin D. Coward, Mere, Wiltshire

Peter R. Coward, Baltimore, USA

Richard and Karen Coward, Mere, Wiltshire

Richard P. Coward, Mere, Wiltshire

Robert Coward, Fleet, Hampshire

Rodney and Shirley Coward, Mere, Wiltshire

Shirley A. Coward, Mere Down – 1st June 1935

Simon D. Coward, Walton-on-Thames

Susan Coward, Winchester, Hampshire

David and Ann Cowley, Burrygreen, Gower, Wales

John A. Cox

Patricia Croteau (née Stone), Garson, Ontario, Canada

Janet E. Crumpton, Mere, Wiltshire

Caleb and Mary Curtis (née Maidment), Mere, Wiltshire (left Wiltshire in 1860s)

Anna Czemerda, Portsmouth, Hampshire

Andrew and Vibeke Dawson, Mere, Wiltshire

Betty Annie May Dean

Ruth Dennett (née Coward), Mere, Wiltshire

Mr Chriss Deverill, Patchway, Bristol

Michael L. Doddington, Mere, Wiltshire

Duchy Manor School, Mere, Wiltshire

Peter and Pat Durkee

Flavia Ebbisham, Mere, Wiltshire

Karen and Jon Edkins, Mere, Wiltshire

The Rev Ben Elliott, Harnham, Salisbury, Wiltshire

The Revd W.H.V. and Mrs E.J. Elliott, Salisbury

Mrs Gail Eyre (née Hinchliffe), St Agnes, Cornwall

David, Carol and Simon Farnfield, Mere

Suzanne Farrington, Lower Zeals

Marilyn Flack (née Bristow), Cheltenham, Gloucestershire

Bethan and Richard Fletcher, Mere, Wiltshire

Dennis, Barbara and Jacqueline Flexney-Briscoe

Mrs Evelyn C. Flower

Sylvia M. Flower, Mere, Wiltshire

Phyllis M. Forbes, Great Eccleston, Lancashire

Simon J. Ford, Mere, Wiltshire

Stan Ford, Southbrook, Mere

Patrick John Fricker, Mere, Wiltshire

Margaret A. Fricker, Mere, Wiltshire

Stephen and Barbara Gale, North Road, Mere, Wiltshire

John D. Gatehouse, Swindon

Neil A. Gatehouse, Dorchester

Peter K. Gatehouse, Mere

Bryan Gordon-Smith, Yew Glen, Mere, Wiltshire

Bernice Greenslade, Mere, Wiltshire

Nicholas Guy, Mere, Wiltshire

Gwen Guy and Alan Johnson, Mere, Wiltshire

Eric and Terry Hall, Andover

Linda Harry (née Bristow), Horsham, Sussex

June H. Harvell, Broadhembury, Honiton, Devon

Miss Pamela A. Hawkings

Clive Hazzard

David and Carole Higgs, Bedford

Tim, Toni, Philip and Sarah Higgs, Mere, Wiltshire

David Hill and Louise, Water Street, Mere

Mark and Sarah Hill, Boar Street, Mere

Paul and Wendy Hill, Water Street, Mere

Pearl Ann Hill (née Fricker), Mere, Wiltshire

Raymond and Valerie Hill and Alfie Jones, Elmwood House, Mere

Heather Hillier, Mere, Wiltshire

Roger Hillman, Duchy Manor School, Mere

Joy and Doug Hills, Castlebridge, Mere, Wiltshire

Pam Hinchliffe (née Norris)

Ruth (widow), Barbara and Dawn (daughters) Hitchings, of the late Reg Hitchings

Mr and Mrs Hollindale, Mere

Maggie Holmes (née Read), Stourbridge

Mr Richard Kenneth Hooper, 'Terra-Firma', Mere

Richard Hopkins, 'Hurdles'

Ted Horan, Mere, Wiltshire

Irene Horlock (née Avery), Shaftesbury, Dorset

John Penn Howard, Mere, Wiltshire

Irene Howe, Mere, Wiltshire

Mr J.E. Howe, Mere, Wiltshire

Bernard and Adrienne Howell, Mere

John and Isabel Howell, Mere, Wiltshire

Susan J. Hunt (née Sheppard), Milton-on-Stour, Dorset

Alexandra Jane Hurd, born Mere, 1 May 1986

Gary and Liz Ings, Mere, Wiltshire

Gordon and Thelma Ings, Mere, Wiltshire

P. and J. Isom

Gordon Jackson, Zeals, Wiltshire

George Edwin Jeans, Mere, Wiltshire

Revd K.E. Kendra OBE, formerly of Mere

Miss Anne Lander, Mere, Wiltshire

Dr Michael Lander, Plymouth, Devon

David and Kathy Langhorne, Mere, Wiltshire

Mr Roger Lark, Mere, Wiltshire

Alan and Anne Lawrence, La Valle, Wisconsin, USA

John (Jack) Lawrence, Mere, Wiltshire

Grace Lawrence Wines, Mere

Mr G.M. Lillie

Jill Loader (née Burden & Howell), Mere

John Longbourne

Sallie Lynch (née Bristow), Hampton, West London

Peter L. Mason, Mere, Wiltshire

Anthony K. McCann, Mere, Wiltshire

Evelyn May Mead (née Hill) – the late, Mere, Wiltshire

Eileen McCann (née Mills), Mere, Wiltshire

Paul and Jane Millard, Mere, Wiltshire

J. Mills, Mere, Wiltshire

Leslie R.V. Mitchell, Zeals, Wiltshire

Mrs Gill Morgan, Maidenhead

A. M. Morgan Rees, Mere, Wiltshire

Andrew Murrison MP, House of Commons

Mahesh and Joanna Nair, Pestalozzi Village, East Sussex

Josephine Nicholls (née Chalke), Doulting, Somerset

Mr and Mrs A.S. Norris, St Agnes, Cornwall

Mrs Odette Norris, Mere, Wiltshire

Charles Edward Nurse, Trevordale, Causeway, Mere

Constance O'Farrell, MBE, Mere, Wiltshire

Claire Osborne (née Chalke), Merced, California, USA

Mr Sidney Palmer, Lower Zeals

Mr Fredrick T. Parfitt, Mere, Wiltshire

Mary Pay (née Bristow), Southwell, Nottinghamshire
Audrey Peers, Bourton, Dorset
Anne Pester (née Dennett), Mere, Wiltshire
Monica Pester, Mere, Wiltshire
Gladys W. Pope
Mr and Mrs A. Porter, Mere, Wiltshire
Anne Preston-Littlewood, Monksilver, Somerset
Rosemary Price, Mere, Wiltshire
B.H. and P.N. Ralph, Burton
Jean and Owen Rees, Mere
Mr and Mrs G. Riddick, North Road, Mere
Vaughn and Sarah Riddick, Black Lawn, Gillingham, Dorset
Beatrice May Wiltshire Ridgley, Gillingham, Dorset
Jean, Jose, Jose Jr., Jane Rodriguez, Mere, Wiltshire
Gillian and Clive Rogers, Wincanton, Somerset
Mr and Mrs Fenton Rutter
Mr Frederick John Sams
Brynley F. Sheppard, Mere, Wiltshire
Reginald A. Sheppard, Mere, Wiltshire
B.A. Shotter, Mere, Wiltshire
Ann and Roy Sims, Castle Street, Mere
Helen J. Smart (née Welch), Risca, Gwent
Gerald W. (John) Snook, Mere, Wiltshire
Graham Spalding, Herne Bay, Kent
Ann Sparkes
Robert and Julie Spencer, Beaufort, Ebbw Vale, Wales
Louis and Sarah Stanton, Woodlands, Mere
Mr and Mrs C.J. Stephenson, Mere, Wiltshire
Angela Stoddart
Paula, Trevor and Scott Stone, Mere, Wiltshire
Joan M. Sutton, Mere, Wiltshire
Mr and Mrs Jeremy Symonds, Mere, Wiltshire

Helen Taylor (née Burden), Bristol
Roland Taylor, Blackfield, Hampshire
Tony Taylor, Mere, Wiltshire
Brian and Ruth Thomas, Mere, Wiltshire
Rev J. Thompson
Michael F. Tighe
Ken and Grace Toms, Mere, Wiltshire
Peter and Anne Towndrow, Grazeley Green, Berkshire
S. Fred Tranter, Mere, Wiltshire
Gill and Carl Tunnicliffe, Mere, Wiltshire
Carol Vigars (née Harding), Nuts, Mere, Wiltshire
Yvonne Viner (née Avery), Mere, Wiltshire
John Vye, Southwick, Sussex
Keith and Janet Waghorne, Mere, Wiltshire
The Wakeling Family, Mere, Wiltshire
Irene E. Wallace, Mere, Wiltshire
John F.W. Walling, Newton Abbot, Devon
Warminster Museum
Michael Warren, Mere, Wiltshire
Margaret Wearne (née Hopkins), Castle Street, Mere
Beryl Webb, Mere, Wiltshire
John Welch, Didcot, Berkshire
Mary Whatley, Trowbridge
Richard J. Whatley, Bath
A. John C. White, Charnage
Patricia Whitehead (née Hoskins), Hilperton, Wiltshire
Mrs A.C. Whitney, Mere, Wiltshire
Mr Edgar F.C. Whitty, Mere, Wiltshire
Melvin J. Wilkinson, Mere, Wiltshire
Hilary Willoughby, Mere
Chris and Janet Wood, Mere Fish Farm
Jean Young, Mere, Wiltshire
Terry and Loraine Young, Mere, Wiltshire